Judaism

Major World Religions Series

Donald K. Swearer, Editor

Judaism

BY SAMUEL T. LACHS, Ph.D., and
SAUL P. WACHS, Ph.D.

Argus Communications
A Division of DLM, Inc.
Niles, Illinois U.S.A.

PHOTO CREDITS

Braun/ALPHA PHOTO ASSOCIATES 66
Werner Braun/FREE LANCE PHOTOGRAPHERS GUILD 90
Eric Carle/SHOSTAL ASSOCIATES 30
John Cumming cover: middle right
B. D. Finley/FREE LANCE PHOTOGRAPHERS GUILD 14
Leonard Freed/MAGNUM PHOTOS 27
Goldman/ALPHA PHOTO ASSOCIATES 46
W. Gontschaross/SHOSTAL ASSOCIATES 70
Lew Gordon 11
Tamar Grand 23, 54, 79, 86
Charles Harbutt/MAGNUM PHOTOS 83
A. Himmelreich/SHOSTAL ASSOCIATES cover: top right
G. Nalbandian/SHOSTAL ASSOCIATES cover: top left
Richard Nowitz/FREE LANCE PHOTOGRAPHERS GUILD 39
SHOSTAL ASSOCIATES cover: bottom left
M. Williams/SHOSTAL ASSOCIATES 3
Courtesy of the Yivo Institute for Jewish Research cover: bottom right

COVER DESIGN

Gene Tarpey

Argus Communications
A Division of DLM, Inc.
7440 Natchez Avenue
Niles, Illinois 60648 U.S.A.

International Standard Book Number: 0-89505-023-4

Library of Congress Number: 79-53060

0 9 8 7 6 5 4 3 2

Contents

Foreword

"The study of religion is the study of mankind." Religion touches the deepest feelings of the human heart and is part of every human society. In modern times religion has been studied by sociologists and anthropologists as a cultural institution. Psychologists see religion as an expression of an inner human need. Philosophers view it as a system of thought or doctrine. Historians consider religion a part of the intellectual and institutional development of a given era.

What is religion? Modern definitions range from "what man does in his solitude" to "an expression of collective identity," and from "man's experience of awe and fascination before a tremendous mystery" to "projective feelings of dependency." The scope of life that religion is identified with is so vast, and the assumptions about the nature of religion are so varied, that we may readily agree with those who say that the study of religion is the study of mankind.

Religion takes many forms, or perhaps it would be better to say that there are many aspects to religion. They include *belief* (e.g., the belief in a creator God), *ritual action* (e.g., making offerings to that God), *ethical action* (following God's law), the formation of *religious communities,* and the formulation of *creeds and doctrinal systems.*

Joachim Wach, a scholar of religion, has pictured religion in terms of religious experience which expresses itself in thought, action, and fellowship.[1] In this view religion is rooted in religious experience, and all other aspects of religion are expressions of that experience. For example, the Buddha's experience of the highest Truth (in Buddhism called *Nirvana*) led him to teach what he had experienced (known as *dharma*) and resulted in the formation of a monastic community (known as *sangha*).

It must be remembered that religions develop within particular historical and cultural traditions and not in a vacuum. This fact has several profound consequences for the study of religion. In the first place it means that religion can never be completely separated from particular historical and cultural traditions. For example, early Christian thought was deeply influenced by both Semitic and Greek traditions, and such central Christian celebrations as Christmas and Easter owe their form to pre-Christian European traditions.

---

[1] Joachim Wach, *The Comparative Study of Religions* (New York: Columbia University Press, 1958).

Furthermore, since a religion is subject to cultural and historical influences, its traditions are always developing relative to particular times and places. For example, the form of worship used in the Buddhist Churches of America (founded in the late nineteenth century) has as much or more in common with American Protestant worship services than with its traditional Japanese form. A religion, then, as part of a specific historical and cultural stream, changes through time and can be fully understood only in relationship to its historical and cultural forms. By way of generalization we might say that Christianity as a religion is only partially understood in terms of its central beliefs and that a fuller or more complete understanding demands a knowledge of its worldwide history and the influence of its various cultural traditions.

In the second place, since a religion develops within particular historical and cultural settings, it also influences its setting. In other words, there is a give-and-take relationship between a religion and its environment. For example, in traditional societies like medieval Europe, Christianity was the inspiration for much of the art and architecture. The same is true for traditional India, where Buddhism and Hinduism decisively affected artistic forms, or for traditional Persia with Islam. Of course, religion influences its environment in other than merely artistic realms. It has had profound effects on modes of behavior (ethics), conceptions of state (politics), forms of economic endeavor—indeed, on all aspects of life.

As a consequence of the pervasive influence of religion in so many aspects of human endeavor, students of religion and society have observed that in traditional societies religion was never isolated. That is, nothing within the given society was perceived as nonreligious or profane. Every meaningful act was seen as religious or sacred. Professor Robert Bellah of the University of California at Berkeley argues that in the West the split between the sacred and the profane or the differentiation of religion from other aspects of life did not really begin until about the time of the Protestant Reformation. He refers to that period as "early modern." Beginning with the early modern period onward to the present, religion has become more and more differentiated from Western culture. Thus, for example, it is no longer assumed that an American is a Protestant, whereas it is still largely assumed that a Thai is a Buddhist.

The question has been asked, "Can someone understand a religion in which he or she does not believe?" As the previous discussion of the nature of religion indicates, belief in the truth claims of a religious tradition is not a prerequisite for engaging in its study or even for understanding (i.e., making sense of) its beliefs and historical forms. The study of religion, however, does demand empathy and sympathy. To engage in the study of another religion for the purpose of proving that one's own is superior can only result in a distorted understanding of that tradition. Or, for that matter, if one who professes no religious belief approaches the study of religion with an inhibiting skepticism, then the beauty and richness of religion will be lost. For the believer, the study of another religious tradition should enhance his or her own faith-understanding; for the nonbeliever (i.e., agnostic), the study of religion should open up new dimensions of the human spirit.

The objective study of religion should be undertaken because of its inherent significance—because the understanding of cultures and societies, indeed, of humankind, is severely limited when such study is ignored. The study of our own tradition from its own particular creedal or denominational perspective is justifiably a part of our profession of faith. However, such study should not close us off from a sympathetic understanding of other religious traditions. Rather, such inquiry should open us to what we share in common with other religious persons, as well as to what is genuinely unique about our own religious beliefs and traditions.

Is the study of religion relevant today? The authors of this series believe the answer is a resounding "Yes!" The United States—indeed, the world—is in the midst of a profound transition period. The crisis confronting nations today cannot be reduced merely to economic inflation, political instability, and social upheaval. It is also one of values and convictions. The time has passed when we can ignore our crying need to reexamine such basic questions as who we are and where we are going—as individuals, as communities, and as a nation. The interest in Islam on the part of many American blacks, experimentation with various forms of Asian religions by the "Age of Aquarius" generation, and a resurgence of Christian piety on college campuses are particular responses to the crisis of identity through which we are currently passing.

The serious study of religion in the world today is not only legitimate but necessary. Today we need all of the forces we can muster in order to restore a sense of individual worth, moral community, and value direction. The sympathetic study of religion can contribute toward these goals and can be of assistance in helping us to recover an awareness of our common humanity too long overshadowed by our preoccupation with technological and material achievement. As has been popularly said, we have conquered outer space at the expense of inner space.

But why study non-Western religions? The reason is quite simple. We no longer live in relative isolation from the cultures of Asia and Africa. As a consequence the marketplace of ideas, values, and faiths is much broader than it used to be. We are in contact with them through popular books and the news media, but for the most part our acquaintance is superficial at best. Rather than looking at the religions imbedded in these cultures as quaint or bizarre—an unproductive enterprise—we should seek genuine understanding of them in the expectation of broadening, deepening, and hopefully clarifying our own personal identity and direction. The study of religion is, then, a twofold enterprise: engaging the religion(s) as it is, and engaging ourselves in the light of that religion.

The Argus Communications Major World Religions Series attempts to present the religious traditions of Judaism, Christianity, Islam, Hinduism, Buddhism, China, and Africa in their unity and variety. On the one hand, the authors interpret the traditions about which they are writing as a faith or a world view which instills the lives of their adherents with value, meaning, and direction. On the other hand, each volume attempts to analyze a particular religion in terms of its historical and cultural settings. This latter dimension means that the authors are interested in the present form of a religious tradition as well as its past development. How can Christianity or Judaism speak to the problems confronting Americans today? What are some of the new religions of Africa, and are they displacing traditional beliefs and world views? Can Maoism be considered the new religion of China? Is traditional Hinduism able to cope with India's social, economic, and political change? The answers to such questions form a legitimate and important part of the content of the series.

The author of each volume is a serious student and teacher of the tradition about which he or she is writing. Each has spent considerable time in countries where that religious tradition is part of the culture. Furthermore, as individuals, the authors are committed to the positive value the proper study of religion can have for students in these times of rapid social, political, and economic change. We hope that the series succeeds in its attempt to present the world's religions not as something "out there," a curiosity piece of times past, but as a subject of study relevant to the needs of our times.

Part I

History of Judaism

From the point of view of *Halakhah* (Jewish law), a Jew is someone who is born to a Jewish mother or who converts to Judaism. This definition, accepted by the overwhelming majority of knowledgeable Jews, gives structure and order to the life of the individual Jew and to Jewish group existence. More than other religions, Judaism is the religion of a particular people. To be a Buddhist, a Muslim, a Christian, or a Hindu does not, in and of itself, mean that an individual is thereby part of a particular ethnic or national grouping. To be a Jew, however, is to be a member of the Jewish people. It is in this light that one can understand the great sense of corporate concern that has always marked Jews around the world. They are bound by a bond that is ethnic and national, as well as spiritual. Israel is seen by them as a national home and as a spiritual center.

Throughout history, the people who are known as Jews today have been called by various names—Hebrews, Israelites, and Jews. The Hebrews were one of a group of Semitic peoples that included the Israelites. The origin of the word *Hebrew* is shrouded in obscurity. It may bear some relationship to the word *Habiru* or *Hapiru,* a wandering Semitic group. We can only say that the Hebrews originated in the ancient Near East, in an area where North-West Semitic was spoken. The earliest reference to the Hebrews is found in the Bible. Sometime at the beginning of the second pre-Christian millenium, Abraham, father of the group, led them from ancient Mesopotamia to the land of Canaan. The Torah recounts that he and the other patriarchs, Isaac and Jacob, were promised by God that their descendants would inherit this land forever.

1

But the move was far more significant than a change in locale. The very characteristics of the group changed along with the geographical move. The emerging characteristics were (1) ethical monotheism—a belief in one God whose essence is morality, (2) the concept that this God had made a covenant, or *Berit,* with the patriarchs, and (3) the concretization of the *Berit* through the rite of circumcision. The sagas of the patriarchs from Abraham to Moses are written in the form of "ancient history," that is, historical experience embellished by legend and cultural stories. Therefore, from a historical point of view, one more correctly speaks of the origin of the Jewish people with Moses and the Exodus (ca. 1220 B.C.E.). The patriarchal period ended with Jacob's descent into Egypt prompted by a famine in Canaan. Subsequently his descendants were enslaved by the Egyptians and remained in slavery for more than four hundred years.

EGYPT AND THE EXODUS

Despite the almost complete lack of nonbiblical material relating to the subject of their sojourn in Egypt, there is very little doubt that the Jews were slaves in that land and that they left there for the Promised Land. The fact is that people do not create for themselves a slave ancestry; they are more likely to want to create an ancestry of nobility than to acknowledge slave origins.

Interestingly, the Exodus was seen as only the first part of a continuing experience which was to end with the conquest of and settlement in the Promised Land. The high point of this experience was seen as having taken place at Mount Sinai where the Torah (the Law) was revealed. Exactly what took place at Sinai we do not know, but we can say that from its earliest period, Jewish tradition preserved the memory of an experience that represented the renewal of the *Berit,* or covenant, between God and Israel. Furthermore, tradition connected this experience of covenantal renewal with the Law. The Law, then, was seen as being a key part of the birth or rebirth of the people. Since the Law was always attributed to divine authorship, the result was the perception of a threefold relationship of God-Torah-Israel (the people) that was to suffuse Jewish tradition from that day and throughout Jewish history.

A sculpture of Moses
in the Bezalel Museum in Jerusalem.

CONQUEST AND SETTLEMENT IN CANAAN

From the patriarchal period, the Children of Israel maintained a tradition of proprietary rights over the land. Even the sojourn in Egypt was part of this tradition since the Egypt experience was seen as directly related to the presence of a famine in the land of Canaan (Genesis 12:10–20; 42:1–50:26). Historically speaking, the conquest of Canaan was a long process. It began with the period of Joshua, successor of Moses (late thirteenth and early twelfth centuries) and continued after his death. The land was populated and divided according to the tribes. While all of these tribes maintained a loose connection, two distinct groupings emerged, one among the ten northern tribes and the other among the two southern tribes of Judah and Benjamin. This latter grouping remained important during the following centuries. During this period central leadership disappeared. This was the period of the judges, a time when leadership was local and charismatic. Many of the stories in the Book of Judges tell of crises brought about by foreign invasion in which the people turned to a private citizen and entrusted him or her with temporary leadership in order to defend themselves against the external threat. With the end of each crisis, the leader more often than not returned to private or semi-private life. A key point in understanding these stories is that, almost without exception, the leadership was exercised over a *portion* of the tribes, not the entire grouping.

CREATION OF THE KINGDOM

Samuel, the last of the judges and the first of the prophets of Israel, was unhappy with the Jewish people's demand for a king, seeing this as a rejection of the Kingship of God. Ultimately he bowed to their demands, and Saul, a young man of the tribe of Benjamin, was chosen.

An able military leader, Saul united the tribes and began to relieve the pressure of the Philistines, who constituted a serious threat to Israelite independence. But he was unable to sustain his place. Afflicted with extreme moodiness and aware that Samuel was ambivalent about the monarchy, he gradually lost his effectiveness. Another young man, David, son of Jesse and a gifted musician, became part of the king's entourage, charged with the responsibility of soothing the king. His popularity grew after he defeated Goliath, a Philistine hero. Saul's strong but mixed feelings toward David intensified when his son Jonathan became David's closest friend. Gradually Saul began to see David as a threat, so that eventually David had to flee. Pursued by Saul again and again, David was forced to live as an outlaw together with other outcasts. Ultimately Saul and Jonathan fell in battle as Israel was overwhelmed by the Philistines. In 1006 B.C.E., the last of Saul's sons was assassinated, and all of the tribes accepted David as king.

David founded a dynasty that was to survive for hundreds of years. He was considered to be the king par excellence. His reputation rested on charisma, talent, religious fervor, military genius, and statesmanship. He united the tribes during his reign, subdued all the neighboring tribes and nations that had periodically warred with the people, broke the power of the Philistines, and expanded the borders of Israel. One of his major acts was to create a capital that would be a national center for the Jewish people. He chose Jerusalem, whose location made it a natural meeting place for the northern and southern tribes.

When David died at the end of a long reign, the kingdom passed into the hands of his son Solomon. The realm that Solomon inherited was strong, united, and at peace, so that he was free to apply his efforts entirely to building and embellishing it. The new king constructed palaces and increased trade between Israel and its neighbors. His fleets exchanged products with African nations, India, and Arabia. In the arts, commerce, and industry, he secured important relationships with neighboring rulers. Because he was not a warrior, Solomon preferred to enhance his kingdom through political alliances. Following a popular practice, the king cemented these alliances through marriage to the daughters of other kings. Utilizing the labor of his subjects and inspired by the palaces he saw during his visits to other capitals, he gradually transformed Jerusalem into an impressive, cosmopolitan center.

Of all his works, the one which was most impressive and meant the most to his people was Solomon's Temple. Constructed originally as a royal chapel, the Temple became the great national and religious shrine of the Jewish people. Its dedication was a major event described in detail in the Bible. This great religious center, destroyed and rebuilt more than once, became and remains the most sacred and revered spot on earth for Jews the world over. Its importance as a symbol was never lost, and its remnant (the famed Western Wall) is, to this day, a favorite gathering place for Jews to worship. Thus Solomon, through his program of construction and alliance, raised his kingdom to a level of international importance.

But this massive program of construction and the expenditure of vast sums to achieve royal splendor resulted in the reawakening of regional and local grievances among the people. These burst into the open after Solomon's death and resulted in the permanent split of the tribes into the earlier groupings. Now, however, they emerged as two distinct countries—Israel and Judah. While the southern country—Judah—retained its loyalty to the House of David, the northern country—Israel—underwent an ongoing experience of political instability. Dynasty followed dynasty with great frequency, often marked by violence. Israel was not able to maintain itself, and by 722 B.C.E. it was destroyed by a superpower, Assyria. The southern kingdom of Judah continued intact under Davidic rulers until it was conquered by the Babylonians. In 586 B.C.E., after unsuccessful attempts at revolt, the Temple was destroyed and many of the people were exiled to the land of the victors.

Having briefly reviewed the political history of the Jewish people during the First Kingdom, it now remains to say a word about the leadership of the people. While the political leadership was in the hands of kings, the cultic worship was presided over by a priesthood that traced its beginnings to Aaron, brother of Moses. The priests were assisted by Levites in the conduct of temple worship. In addition to these groups of ongoing leadership, there arose from time to time, particularly from the eighth century B.C.E. onward, men and women known as prophets who were seen as messengers of God. These prophets, or *Nevi-im* (singular: *Navi*), acted as the conscience of the people, calling the people or their leaders to task for lapses in the observance of the law, particularly the moral law. Although they came from different strata of society, the prophets shared certain common elements:

1. Each saw himself or herself as a vehicle for the transmission of God's word.
2. Each left a personal message, rooted in the idea of the *Berit,* or covenant.
3. Each saw the essence of the people's responsibility as living in accordance with God's law.

The prophetic message had two components. On the one hand, the prophets condemned injustice in harsh terms. On the other hand, they offered comfort and hope to the people. What is striking in the prophetic message is that, despite the national concerns of the prophets and their obvious concern for a particular people, their words seem to have universal meaning and have come to hold tremendous significance to people of many cultures and ages. It is also striking that the prophets seem to have enjoyed, in the main, a remarkable immunity that allowed them to speak openly even when castigating the king (for example, II Samuel 12, I Kings 21). There was a unique sensitivity among the people toward the prophets. From king to the ordinary citizen, there was an awareness that each prophet represented a link between the people and God and that his or her voice was the voice of truth. This acceptance of the legitimacy of prophetic articulation of the covenant seems all the more impressive when one recalls the fate of social critics in the ancient world and in our own day.

BABYLONIAN CONQUEST

In order to understand the basis of the Babylonian captivity, one must understand the rationale for ethnic or national captivity in general. In the ancient world, as large empires such as those of Assyria and Babylonia developed, it was deemed valuable by those empires to be selective in transplanting conquered populations. Upon defeating a people, the victors would take away the best educated and leading members of the defeated society, thus removing those elements that would be most likely to provide leadership for a revolt among the conquered people.

Unquestionably, the exile that took place in the beginning of the sixth century B.C.E. was a tremendous challenge to Jewish survival. This was the first time since the conquest of the land by Joshua that large numbers of Jews had been uprooted from it. To live in Diaspora (dispersion) meant to live without key religious norms of Jewish life, such as the Temple and sacrificial cult. With the exception of the experience of the Jews in Babylonia, there is no example in the ancient world of a people who was able to preserve its identity in exile. In view of subsequent Jewish history, it is most interesting to analyze what actually happened. The following chronology is intended to provide a brief summary of the exile.

In 597 B.C.E., the first group of Jewish leaders was carried away in an unsuccessful effort to forestall a revolt against Babylonia. In 586 B.C.E., the conquest of Jerusalem, together with the destruction of Solomon's Temple, was followed by the exile of a larger group of Jews. In 538 B.C.E., having defeated the Babylonians, Cyrus the Great, king of Persia, issued an edict permitting the Jews to return home; but, a relatively small number—less than fifty thousand people—responded. By 516 B.C.E., the Second Temple, a much more modest effort than its predecessor, was built and a small and fragile Jewish life was under way again in the ancient homeland of Judea. Beset with attacks by their neighbors, the Samaritans, and always in danger of being considered disloyal to their Persian overlords, the community was dispirited until a second wave of return and the strong leadership of Ezra and Nehemiah (444 B.C.E.) reinstituted a sense of forward direction and vitality among the small Jewish community (see the books of Ezra and Nehemiah).

What is interesting about this period, so crucial in Jewish experience, is that almost nothing is known about what actually took place. We are forced to deal with it through conjecture. Outside of the account given in the Bible, the historian can approach the subject only by asking the question, What changes took place in Jewish life in Judea after the return that might be attributed to the influence of the Babylonian experience? In other words, in noting the appearance of certain aspects of Jewish life after the return that were not present before the exile, it may be conjectured that these new developments reflect the experience of the seventy years in Babylonia. For example, the beginning of a Jewish doctrine of an afterlife can be traced to the period following the Babylonian captivity. In the material available before that time, no such concept is to be found. It is possible (though by no means definite) that the introduction of this concept (for example, in the Book of Daniel) is a result of the Jewish experience of exile among the Babylonians and Persians.

Another and even more important new development in Jewish life was the synagogue. While scholars are not agreed as to the details of the beginnings of this institution, the preponderance of scholarly opinion would place those beginnings in the period of the Second Temple. This may well suggest the influence of the Babylonian experience where the absence of the Temple and a sacrificial cult created a religious vacuum that may have led to the eventual development of "small sanctuaries" among the dispersed groups of Jews.

It is also assumed that while in Babylonia the Jewish community accepted the leadership of the priesthood without a temple. Hopes for a restoration of Jewish life in the homeland were kept alive by the priestly prophet Ezekiel (see Ezekiel 37, for example, for a famous example of prophetic hopes). After the first wave of Jews returned to the Promised Land (539 B.C.E.), the leadership of the community was eventually assumed by the priests. It may be said, then, that from this time until the Maccabean revolt (168 B.C.E.), the Jews were ruled over by priests and Jewish life was a theocracy, with the *Kohen Gadol,* or high priest, serving as both religious and secular leader.

Perhaps the most important of the new developments in Jewish life that seem to be related to the Babylonian captivity is what may be called the introduction of religious egalitarianism into Jewish life. This development can be attributed to a new learned class that emerged during the period of exile. Unlike the priests, this class was not limited to a particular family or tribe but was open to all. Moreover, through the regular practice of public study of the Law, or Torah, the way was open to greater participation of the common people in religious life. While the priests and Levites retained conduct of the cultic life in the Temple, religious life became increasingly egalitarian, that is, open for participation and leadership among all elements of the people. In the beginning of the period following the return, the priests probably continued to dominate the process of teaching the Law, as they had in the past (Malachi 2:7). But now, participation in Torah study became a matter of choice and ability unrelated to lineage or rank among the people. Ezra's role in this process is crucial (Ezra 7:10). Upon his return to Judea in 444, Ezra arranged for a major convocation of the people (Nehemiah 8) in which the Law was read and explained. From this we may assume that he reflected, at least to some extent, ideas and developments that were current in the exile experience.

Moreover, the Law took on a new importance and became the constitution of the Jewish people, to be studied and expounded as the normative guide for living. All future generations saw the Law as the source of Jewish life. The study of the Torah took on a greater importance, and all of the sacred literature that developed in later years was directly or indirectly seen as nothing but a commentary on the "constitution."

This development in Jewish life also marked the end of prophecy among the Jews. In the past, God's will was believed to be made known to the people through the prophets; now it was seen as being directly available to them through the Torah. With the Torah becoming paramount in Jewish religion, the need for teachers of the Law replaced the need for charismatic "voices of God."

As a result of these experiences, the Jews became increasingly universalistic in outlook; or, more correctly, those universalistic tendencies in the ancient religion of Israel were strengthened. As the Jews underwent successive periods of political control by Persians, Greeks, and Romans, they came to see themselves as part of a larger (world) civilization. This inevitably led to the rise of conflicting philosophies among Jews as to how one was to live Jewishly and yet participate in the larger culture of the then-known world. Three distinct groups within the Jewish community can be identified, each of which espoused a different philosophy of Judaism.

First of all, there were the priests, or *Kohanim* (singular: *Kohen*). These were allied with the wealthy and landed aristocracy. Their view is best described as conservative in matters of religion. Believing in a rather strict or narrow interpretation of the Torah, they could not, for example, accept a belief in the "world to come" because they could find no basis for the belief in the Torah. This group became known as the Sadducees, a name which some authorities believe is taken from Zadok, the high priest under King Solomon and founder of the priestly family that had dominated the priesthood for centuries (I Kings 2:35).

A second group was called Separatists (in Hebrew, *Perushim,* or Pharisees). They represented a much larger segment of the population of Judea, particularly among the middle and lower classes. This group felt that if Judaism were to keep pace with the changes in society, there would have to be a broader interpretation of the Torah. The vehicle for this broader interpretation was the Oral Law (Hebrew: *Torah She-beal Peh*), the interpretations of the Torah that had been developed by those who sought in each generation to apply the Jewish tradition to the problems of daily living. The Pharisees were the forerunners of the rabbis, and their approach to the Torah and to the tradition proved to be normative for Judaism. The Pharisees and the rabbis sought to uncover the deeper meaning and purpose of the Torah and to preserve its vitality as a humanizing force within Jewish life.

In addition to the Sadducees and the Pharisees, a third group—the Essenes—emerged during the latter part of the Second Temple period. The Essenes were a small monastic or semimonastic group who separated themselves from both the Sadducees and the Pharisees and lived an isolated existence in the land of Judea. Today, many scholars identify the Essenes with the "Covenanters" of the Dead Sea Scrolls.

GREEK AND ROMAN RULE

With the rise of Alexander the Great (356–323 B.C.E.), a new period began for the Jews. The lightning victories of the young Alexander placed an enormous amount of territory under his control, including almost all of the Jewish world. Alexander's policy toward the lands that he conquered was to leave the inner life of the land, including its religion, virtually untouched and to content himself with political control. The people of Judea did not resist his invasion and were treated rather well by Alexander. Now, for the first time, Jews became exposed to western (Greek) ideas. These ideas were, in many ways, fundamentally different from the bases of Judaism. Jewish egalitari-

Site of the Qumran caves where
the Dead Sea Scrolls were found.
The Dead Sea is seen in the background.

anism *under the Law* was unknown in Greece; and Jewish concepts of morality, such as the treatment of foreigners and slaves and a commitment to marital fidelity, contrasted strongly with those found among the Greeks. Most important, Jewish ethical monotheism was totally opposed to the type of polytheistic paganism that dominated the religious life of the Greeks. The contact of Jews and Greeks created new tensions within the Jewish community, with some Jews being attracted by Greek ideas and practices and others being totally repelled by what they saw to be a threat to the Jewish religion. The resultant tensions led eventually to the Maccabean revolt, which is discussed in the section on Hanukkah (pp. 87–88).

When the Maccabean revolt had run its course, Judea was in the hands of the Hasmonean family (141 B.C.E.), and so it continued throughout the balance of the second century B.C.E. and into the middle of the first. While the first Hasmoneans maintained the idealism that had sparked the Maccabean revolt, those who followed them did not; and the gradual degeneration of the monarchy led to the creation of a sense of alienation between the ruling house and the people of Judea.

Gradually, Judea passed into the Roman orbit as Rome supplanted Greece as the leading power in the eastern Mediterranean world. In 63 B.C.E., Pompey, the Roman conqueror, made Syria a Roman province. Intervening in a dispute between two Hasmonean brothers, he chose one of these—Hyrcanus—as king of Judea. When Aristobulus, the other brother, refused to accept the verdict, Pompey brought his legions to Jerusalem and, after a three-month seige, broke into the city, massacring twelve thousand Jews. Although Hyrcanus was officially king of Judea, Antipater, an Idumean, was left with a controlling voice in the nation's affairs. As Rome's leaders changed (Pompey, Julius Caesar, Mark Anthony, and Octavian), Judea more and more came under the firm control of Rome. In 37 B.C.E., Herod, son of Antipater and a Roman favorite, was declared king of the Jews. As an outsider with no connection to the traditional House of David, Herod was hated by the people he ruled. In an attempt to soften this attitude, he married Mariamne of the Hasmonean family. Driven by the knowledge that he was despised and by an acute paranoia, he exterminated all remnants of the Hasmonean family (including his wife, their sons, and all his wife's relatives) together with other leaders of the Jews.

Herod had a passion for building and constructed many impressive monuments, palaces, fortresses, and temples. His expansion and rebuilding of the Jerusalem Temple made it a truly magnificent edifice. All of this did not soften the enmity of the Jews. The thirty-three years of his rule (37–4 B.C.E.) are recalled in Jewish literature with horror and sadness. The day of his death was the occasion for relief and joy in all of Judea.

The period following Herod's death saw Judea reduced to the status of a Roman province governed by a succession of procurators, each of whom was interested in amassing his own wealth and keeping the Judeans in order. Any effort at gaining freedom from the Romans was met with brutality. Thousands of Jews perished at the hands of the Roman soldiers. Rome was puzzled as to how to deal with the Judeans. Basically committed to a hands-off policy where the people were concerned, it was satisfied with political control and the payment of taxes into its treasuries. It could not fully grasp the essence of the Jewish religion which was so different from the religions of other peoples within the empire. As emperor followed emperor (Tiberius, Caligula, Claudius, Nero), conditions worsened in Judea. Frequent clashes between the people and the Roman soldiers were triggered by the presence of Roman symbols considered by Jews as idolatrous.

In 66 C.E., a full-scale revolt broke out. It was a hopeless effort from the start. The Essenes and many of the Pharisees opposed the fight, reasoning that as long as the religious life of the country was basically allowed to exist, no effort should be made to shake off Roman rule. The Zealots, however, were anxious to fight despite the great odds against them. In 70 C.E., the Roman armies entered Jerusalem, destroyed the Temple, and slaughtered a large part of the population of Jerusalem.

The years following the destruction of the Temple were difficult ones for the Jews. From time to time, their hopes for freedom spurred them to revolt, but each such effort was suppressed. In 117 C.E., during the reign of the Emperor Tragan, a revolt was put down with wholesale slaughter. The climax of this on-again-off-again effort to gain freedom in Judea came in 132 C.E. under Emperor Hadrian. A revolt was triggered when Hadrian sought to eliminate the ritual circumcision, which he categorized as a "barbarous" practice. Whereas earlier revolts had primarily political goals, this revolt was aimed at defending the Jewish religion and thus involved all segments of the Jewish population of Palestine.

Rome won the three-year war, but not without great sacrifices. Furious over the costs, Rome ravaged Judea, turned Jerusalem into a pagan city, and forbade Jews to live anywhere in sight of their lost capital. Thousands of Jews were sold into slavery or martyred. Thousands more fled the land to join their brothers in the Diaspora. Schools and synagogues were closed, and the practice of the Jewish religion was forbidden. Only with the death of Hadrian in 138 C.E. was there any reconciliation between Rome and the Jews. Under

Antoninus Pius, Hadrian's successor, the persecution ended and Jewish religious life was allowed to proceed without interference.

BREAK WITH CHRISTIANITY

Christianity began as a sect within Judaism. Sharing many beliefs of contemporary Jews, its adherents differed essentially from them in the belief that the Messiah—the longed-for redeemer who would rescue the people from their vassal status and restore the homeland to its former glory—had in fact already come in the person of Jesus of Nazareth. It should be stressed, however, that Jesus' followers saw themselves as being part of the people of Israel. They saw themselves as being faithful to the spirit of the Jewish tradition, as embodied in the Bible. They felt themselves to be the true heirs of this tradition, the true Israel. To them, the coming of Jesus represented the fulfillment of God's promises to Abraham. The vast majority of the Jews, however, did not accept this belief, claiming that the Messiah was yet to come. They maintained that when he did come, all of the elements of national degradation—political, social, and economic—would be eliminated and Israel, as a people, would be restored to its former glory under a scion of the House of David.

Seeing that they were making little headway among the Jews, some of the leaders of the Christian community began to spread the gospel ("good news") of Jesus to the Gentiles. Gradually, Christianity turned westward, and Christian activity became centered in the major cities of the Roman Empire—Rome, Antioch, Corinth, Alexandria. Jewish elements in Christianity became less important. As Christians began to reject the concepts of *Halakhah,* peoplehood, and the traditional *Berit* (as symbolized by circumcision), the gulf between the two groups widened.

Christianity became a new religion with no clear ties to Judaism. Its approach became creedal—one of belief rather than one of ethnic concentration. Whereas Judaism had been (and remains) particularistic—that is, the religion of one people—Christianity became universalistic, transcending all boundaries of ethnicity and nationalism. Yet for all of its independence, Christianity clearly asserted its position as the true carrier of the biblical heritage. Feeling the need to explain the

Excavations at the site of the Second Temple.

break with Judaism, while at the same time attaching itself to Jewish history, Christianity declared that Judaism, in rejecting Jesus, was rejecting the biblical tradition. Thus the stage was set for increasing tension between Christians and Jews, since the two groups could not vie for the same heritage and still remain friendly. For many years this tension remained a minor lament in Jewish life; but in the fourth century, Constantine, emperor of Rome, became a Christian, and the Christian religion gradually gained legitimacy and then preference in the eyes of the emperors. With such acceptance, increasing pressures were mounted by Christian leaders to curtail and, where possible, to eliminate the rights of Jewish people and the practice of their religion. This development provides a major (if not the major) reason for the decline of Palestine as a center of Jewish religious life from the fourth century on.

Throughout the following centuries, the fate of the Jews and of the Jewish community hinged on the fragile balance between the Christian Church and the Roman Empire. It should be noted that since the days of Simon the Hasmonean (second century B.C.E.), the Jews had the right of self-determination within the framework of loyalty to the Roman Empire. In the Christian era, this status was referred to as *religio licita,* or an officially recognized religion. This meant that Jews were free to carry on their religious practices without limitation and that they were free from the obligation of emperor worship. Rome honored this status and Jews were allowed to practice their religion; and except for the period of the revolts (see p. 13), the Jews were never persecuted the way the early Christians were.

Only in the fourth century, after the Roman Empire had accepted Christianity, did Jews lose their status. What saved them from cultural and religious extinction was the fact that they were given a new status, that of "servant of the king." As royal "property," they served the king's interests and were at least partially protected from the pressure placed upon them by the Christian Church and its local rulers. This protection remained in effect until the late Middle Ages when the papacy, under Pope Innocent III, achieved domination over the empire. Then, in land after land, the Jews endured persecution and, ultimately, expulsion at the hands of the Christians.

DEVELOPMENT OF THE TALMUD

The years following the destruction of the Temple (70 C.E.) were critical for Jewish survival. At one fell swoop, the Jews had suffered (1) the loss of political freedom, (2) the loss of Jerusalem, and (3) the loss of the Temple and the sacrificial system of worship. That Jewish life did not collapse is largely due to the strength of the Pharisaic institutions, particularly the synagogue and the schools.

After the destruction of the Temple, the Romans permitted Rabbi Johanan ben Zakkai (who had opposed the war with Rome) to gather his disciples and colleagues in a town called Yavneh to continue their studies. Rabbi Johanan soon had reestablished the Sanhedrin, or court, in Yavneh. During the hundred years after the destruction of the Temple, three major tasks were accomplished:

1. The ordering of the Jewish liturgy (ca. 90 C.E.)
2. The completion of the canonization of the Hebrew Bible (ca. 140 C.E.)
3. The development and codification of the Oral Law (ca. 175 C.E.)

From very early times, the written law, or Torah, was interpreted orally. The interpretation was necessary because the Torah, like any law code, speaks tersely. It lays down general principles but does not cover every possible situation in which the law will be invoked. In the wake of the great tragedy of 70 C.E., Rabbi Johanan ben Zakkai and his colleagues, called *Tannaim* (teachers), were faced with a variety of questions from Jews in Palestine and all over the Diaspora. Their discussions were memorized and their decisions gained the force of law. Gradually, the material became too bulky to retain orally.

In the second century, the leader of the Jewish community, Judah Hanasi, made the decision to commit the key decisions of the Oral Law to writing. He divided the materials which he culled into categories (ritual, civil, marital, agricultural, and so on). The resultant work, known as the *Mishnah,* achieved authoritative status all around the Jewish world. Aside from the orderliness of the *Mishnah,* it combined the following features:

1. It included not only the *Halakhah* (law) but often the discussion which accompanied the decision.
2. Minority opinions were also recorded for future reevaluation.
3. The names of authorities supporting various points of view were included, thus adding to the authority of the ideas presented.
4. In addition to the *Halakhot* (laws), the *Mishnah* contained much *Aggadah.* This nonlegal material deals with basic beliefs of Judaism, story material, and religious, ethical, and social thought.

By the year 200 C.E., the *Mishnah* was basically complete. Henceforth, it was to serve as the major textbook for the academies of Jewish scholarship in Palestine and in the Diaspora.

The *Mishnah* was not the only collection of Jewish law produced by the *Tannaim* (70–200 C.E.). Another collection, the *Tosefta,* contained material omitted by the *Mishnah.* Rabbinic sermons, or *Midrashim* (singular: *Midrash*), derived *Halakhah* (law) from the interpretation of biblical verses. But the *Mishnah* achieved the authoritative status as the encyclopedia of *Halakhah.*

It should be noted that because of the work of the *Tannaim,* Palestine was assured of continued recognition as the center of Jewish life. Even in the fourth century, when Jewish life in the Holy Land was seriously weakened, the stronger Diaspora communities (most notably, Babylonia) maintained an attitude of respect toward halakhic (legal) decisions reached by the leaders of the Palestinian community.

Following the redaction of the *Mishnah* (ca. 200 C.E.), a new body of material began to develop. Known as *Gemara,* it represented the minutes of discussions held in the academies of Palestine and Babylonia as scholars studied the *Mishnah* and applied its rulings to daily problems. But now, the condition of Palestinian Jewry continued to deteriorate, and the center of scholarship and authority gradually began to shift to Babylonia. As a result, the Babylonian *Gemara* (completed ca. 550 C.E.) was larger and more comprehensive than the Palestinian *Gemara* (completed ca. 350 C.E.) and thus achieved predominance in Jewish life. Written in Aramaic, an internationally used language, the *Gemara* expounded the *Mishnah* and other tannaitic material. A rich collection of aggadic (nonlegal) material augmented the purely legal material. Taken together, the *Mishnah* and the *Gemara* make up what is known as the Talmud. Because of its richness as the authoritative source of *Halakhah* and Jewish beliefs and values, the (Babylonian) Talmud has remained the subject of intense study to this day. Commentaries have multiplied throughout the generations.

BABYLONIA AND SPAIN

From the eighth to the eleventh century, Jewish life in Babylonia waxed and waned according to the treatment accorded the Jewish community by the reigning authorities. Jewish communal life was headed by an exilarch; religious life was guided by the *Geonim* (literally, "excellencies"), who headed the major academies. The most famous of the *Geonim* was Sa-adiah (892–942), who wrote important works in lexicography, theology, philosophy, poetry, and jurisprudence. His liturgical collection *(Siddur)* is the oldest Jewish prayer book that has survived in its entirety. Much of his life was taken up with an ideological struggle against the Karaites, a group that denied the legitimacy of the Talmud. Reviving ideas associated with the Sadducees, the Karaites called for a very narrow interpretation of the Bible and thus posed a danger to the unity of the Jewish community. Sa-adiah combatted the Karaites in his writings, which proved so effective that rabbinical Judaism was preserved as the normative religious expression among Jews.

With the decline of the Palestinian Jewish community, Jews turned to the *Geonim* of Babylonia for guidance in religious matters. The body of legal correspondence that developed, called responsa literature, formed the basis of later legal compilations. By the middle of the eleventh century, Babylonia ceased to function as an important center of Jewish scholarship and authority. Many Jews, buffeted by economic, political, and religious pressures, left the land. The decline was never to be reversed.

By the year 1050, the center of spiritual gravity among Jews was in Spain. Swelled by emigrants from Babylonia, the ranks of Spanish Jewish scholars, philosophers, lexicographers, and poets grew to the point where important academies were opened and work of enduring value produced.

In general, Jews fared somewhat better under Muslim rule than in Christian lands. Muslims considered Jews to be "People of the Book," that is, holders of an authentic set of revealed scriptures; as such they were entitled to a protected status in society. Occasionally, Jews suffered religious persecution; but, in general, the position of a Jew in Muslim society, while that of a second-class citizen, was reasonably stable and tolerated. Spain proved to be the site of a flowering Judeo-Arabic culture. To this day, Jews call this era a "Golden Age." As in the past, Jews adapted cultural patterns of a friendly host culture. The result was a massive outpouring of Hebrew and Judeo-Arabic works of poetry, prose, grammar, lexicography, rhetoric, philosophy, astronomy, and medicine, together with traditional forms of religious scholarship.

The number of outstanding figures produced in the Golden Age in Spain is far too great to enumerate. Hasdai Ibn Shaprut, for example, acted as adviser to Caliph Abd-ar-Rahman III. A scholar himself, the caliph supported numerous other scholars in the development of many facets of Jewish and general culture. Samuel Hanagid was appointed vizier of Granada in 1025 and was entrusted with the direction of military and diplomatic affairs for a period of thirty years. Of the many outstanding scholarly figures, the greatest was Moses ben Maimon (1135–1204), better known as Maimonides. A physician who fled from a rare instance of Muslim persecution, he found employment as physician to Saladin of Egypt. His remarkable mind produced a series of important works on medicine, philosophy, *Halakhah* liturgy, and other aspects of Jewish religion. His works achieved the status of classics and are studied to this day throughout the world.

Beginning in the fourteenth century, a decline set in. As the power of the Christian Church increased, Jews found their social, economic, and political situation endangered. In 1391, there were massacres. Faced with the choice of baptism or exile or death, for the first time in Jewish history, members of the community decided to join the majority faith. Anti-Jewish laws limited freedom, and the complexion of the Spanish Jewish community changed forever. Now, together with those still clinging to their faith, there were former Jews known as Conversos. Some of these were true Christian believers; others, though they had accepted baptism, continued to practice Judaism in secrecy or else remained Jewish in belief if not in practice. But even the Conversos were not safe. They were often resented by faithful Jews for taking advantage of opportunities that were closed to them. Physical attacks took place. The Conversos were called *Marranos* (swine) by their neighbors.

Meanwhile, pressures on the Jews who resisted baptism intensified. New laws limited their places of residence or form of occupation. Christian sermons were preached in the synagogues, and the Jews were required to listen.

In 1478, a tribunal known as the Inquisition was set up by the Church to ferret out insincere Conversos. Those arrested were often tortured. Those convicted usually faced an "auto-da-fé" (act of faith), or death by fire. The first auto-da-fé took place in 1481. Subsequently thousands of Conversos were burned alive by the Inquisition. Others lost their property and were publicly disgraced. In 1492, Torquemada, inquisitor-general of Spain, convinced Ferdinand and Isabella, wedded monarchs of the newly unified land, that there must be religious unity in Spain. A decree was issued to expel all non-Christians from Spain within four months. Many Jews converted; others pretended to do so. Those who chose to leave their beloved home had to surrender all their property. Of the 150,000 who left, many suffered at the hands of the shipmasters who took them away. What happened in Spain in 1492 also took place in Portugal in 1497. Many *Sefardic* Jews, as the Spanish and Portuguese Jews were called *(Sefarad* is Hebrew for "Spain"), found refuge in Palestine, Holland, Turkey, and, for a time, the Papal States.

In banishing Jews and Muslims, the monarchs of Spain and Portugal achieved religious homogeneity; but in the process, they deprived their lands of creative and energetic people. It is no accident that, by the end of the sixteenth century, Spain and Portugal ceased to be important powers.

In very recent years, Jewish life has begun to revive in Spain and Portugal. Today, small groups of Jews are again free to practice Judaism on the Iberian Peninsula.

MEDIEVAL AND RENAISSANCE EUROPE

While Jews of the Iberian Peninsula were enjoying a "Golden Age," the Jews north of the Pyrenees were also producing important works of scholarship. The difference was one of emphasis. While Spanish Jews wrote works in a variety of areas, the northern Jews concentrated primarily upon talmudic scholarship. Beginning about 1000 C.E., Rabbi Gershom of Mainz developed an important school. This school produced the greatest of all Jewish biblical and talmudic commentators—Rabbi Solomon ben Isaac (1040–1105), better known to Jews by the acronym Rashi. A group known as the *Tosafists,* which included Rashi's grandchildren, added glosses and corrections to the text of the Talmud. To this day, Jewish students of the Bible rely heavily on the commentary of Rashi while texts of the Talmud contain the comments of both Rashi and the *Tosafists.*

This important community of Franco-German Jewry was brutally destroyed during the Crusades. Both on the way to and from their visits to the Holy Land, crusaders raped, looted, forcibly converted, or murdered Jews in Mainz, Speyer, Worms, and other communities. In most cases, Jews were deserted by their neighbors and the local authorities; and when they sought refuge in their synagogue, they perished in the flames as these were burned to the ground. The fervor of the Crusades was responsible for the total destruction of Jewish communities as widely separated as York, England; Blois, France; and Jerusalem, where, in 1099, the main body of crusaders killed the entire Jewish population of the city.

How are we to understand the position of the Jew in Christian Europe? From the time of Constantine to the time of Pope Innocent III at the beginning of the thirteenth century, there was a clash between empire and papacy over the Jews. The kings tended for the most part to deal reasonably with the Jews, seeing in them a source of economic advantage to their lands and to themselves. It is also fair to say that the kings felt some responsibility for them since the Jews were, legally, "servants of the king." The Christian Church, on the other hand, saw in the Jews a living denial of the truth of the Gospel. While they were to be kept alive in order to be able to convert at the return of Jesus, they were entitled to few if any rights and were to be severely limited in their social, political, economic, and religious expression.

As ecclesiastical power grew, the position of the Jews worsened. This power reached its highest point under the papacy of Innocent III (1198–1216). With the barbarians converted and various forms of heresy rooted out, only the Jews stood in the way of a Europe that was essentially all Christian. In 1290, Jews were expelled from England. By the beginning of the sixteenth century, Europe, with the exception of Holland and the Papal States, would be called *Judenrein* ("free of Jews").

From the beginning of the sixteenth century until the French Revolution (1789–1799), Jews did live in Europe but under great disabilities. They were forced to live in ghettos. The ghetto was a segregated portion of a town surrounded by a high wall. Jews could not leave at night nor could Christians enter. Jews were forbidden to employ Christian servants and were barred from almost all professions (medicine was a striking exception). They were often forced to wear a special badge or hat. They could not own real estate. These rules were enforced inconsistently by various rulers and popes. Some, like Pope Paul IV (1555–1559), insisted that Jews be degraded. Others, like the Medici popes Leo X (1513–1521) and Clement VII (1523–1534), encouraged Jewish scholarship as part of the creative outpouring called the Renaissance. Where allowed to do so, Jews participated in this creativity, producing works of music and literature, just as they had done in Muslim Spain.

Books printed in Hebrew first appeared in the fifteenth century. The availability of printed copies of the Hebrew Bible and the Talmud led to uniformity of practice and creed among Jews. It also stimulated an appreciation of Judaism among Christian humanists. Thus when Judaism was attacked in print (often by convert apostates), men like Johann Reuchlin, distinguished German scholar and humanist, defended Judaism in writing. But the attacks of the apostates, however distorted or inaccurate, led to the destruction or censorship of Jewish texts. Only the Bible was safe. The Talmud and liturgy were so tampered with that, to this day, scholars may devote a lifetime of research to trying to reconstruct the text of the Talmud as it was before the censors of the medieval Church had their way with it.

A rabbi studying the Bible with commentaries.

The Middle Ages were a strange and difficult time for Jews. At times, the Christian Church, which worked to banish Jews from other lands, welcomed them into the Papal States. In Italy, Jews functioned as bankers, doctors, and artisans. They taught Hebrew to Christians and discussed their literature with them, particularly the Jewish mystical literature known as *Kabbalah*. But these were more short-lived exceptions than the rule. The Talmud was burned in Rome in 1553; the restrictions were reinstated; and by the middle of the sixteenth century, Italy's Jews were in ghettos.

THE REFORMATION

When Martin Luther (1483–1546) began his campaign to reform the Church, he apparently believed that the Jews' refusal to see the truth of Christianity was a direct result of their persecution. He further believed that by making the Gospel available in Hebrew, the Jews would embrace the Christian faith. When his efforts to convert Jews failed, Luther developed a deep hatred for them. He urged the princes of Protestant Europe to expel them and to destroy their synagogues.

Ironically, some Catholics blamed the Jews for the Reformation. They held that since the reformers were students of Hebrew who advocated making the Bible available to the people, the Reformation was, in effect, the "evil fruit of Jewish influence." The Counter-Reformation led to an increasingly repressive policy against Jews in the Catholic world.

Catholic or Protestant, Europe was, for the most part, a place of extreme hardship for Jews from about 1000 C.E. to the French Revolution. It has been said that for the Jew, the Middle Ages did not end until the end of the eighteenth century, when the gates of the ghetto swung open for good.

EASTERN EUROPE

The beginning of the sixteenth century marks the movement of Jews toward the eastern portions of Europe. Prior to that time, some Jews did move eastward, driven by persecution and attracted by the liberality of Polish rulers. But here again, the pattern repeated itself: royal support and protection of the Jews and persecution by the Church and envious business competitors. As larger numbers of Jews entered Poland, riots took place from time to time, particularly on Christian holy days. Jews were accused of "Blood Libel"—of using human blood as part of their religious practices. They were also charged with causing the Black Death (plague) by poisoning the wells of the communities in which they lived. Thousands of Jews were killed throughout Europe as a result of these accusations.

Yet with all of this, eastern Europe attracted more and more Jews. Here they could participate in mercantile activity, moneylending (forbidden by the Church to Christians), farming, salt mining, fur trading, innkeeping, and many other fields. The community of eastern European Jews became known as the *Ashkenazim* (an ancient name for Germans).

What characterized eastern European Jewish life was its internal organization and self-government. Jews lived according to *Halakhah* without being disturbed. Officers and rabbis were chosen by the community. It also collected taxes for itself and for the government. The great fairs (similar to our own state fairs but held more often) allowed Jews not only to exhibit their wares but also to meet for study and decision making. There developed a "Council of the Four Lands," which acted as a parliament for Polish Jews. With power to tax, to control printing, and to excommunicate, this council represented the strongest and most autonomous government since the days of the exilarch and the *Geonim* of Babylonia.

This period of Jewish autonomy came to a sudden end in 1648, when Ukrainian cossacks revolted against the Poles. The Jews, some of whom acted as managers of property rented by Poles to Ukrainians, were singled out for particular cruelty. The pogroms (riots) matched the brutality of the Crusades. By 1768, Polish Jewry was in ruins. The tide of migration reversed with Jews now turning westward toward central and western Europe to find safety.

MESSIANISM AND HASSIDISM

Although Jewish mystical ideas had existed since the days of the Bible, mystical movements seemed to flourish at times of political, social, and economic hardship. Such a movement was launched in Turkey (you will recall that *Sefardic* Jews were welcomed into Turkey after their expulsion from Spain and Portugal) by Shabbetai Tzevi (1626–1676). Deeply influenced by the literature of *Kabbalah*, Tzevi practiced ascetic mortification and intense religious behavior, believing (as did others) that such behavior would stimulate God to send the long-awaited Messiah. In 1665 this charismatic personality proclaimed himself Messiah and sent letters throughout the world announcing the good news. Rabbis and community leaders were skeptical, but masses of people accepted the news as truth. Believing the agony of Diaspora to be at an end, Jews everywhere sold their possessions and prepared to return to Palestine. At this point, Tzevi set forth for Constantinople. There he was arrested and thrown into prison. Even this did not dismay the bulk of his followers. They believed that the Messiah must suffer before his triumph. In prison, he received thousands of visitors bearing gifts and petitions. Ultimately, the sultan offered him a choice between apostasy and death; and without hesitation, he accepted Islam. Amazingly, many (though not all) of his followers chose to believe that even this was somehow necessary as a temporary prelude to his triumph. Now the Jewish world split. Some persisted in their belief; others were disillusioned. The rabbis now took a dim view of messianic movements, teaching that God would send the Messiah but men should not speculate on the time of his coming.

Touched by the fervor of messianism, some eastern European Jews began to reemphasize the mystical element in Judaism. Israel ben Eliezer (1700–1760), a poor working man of unusual charisma, attracted others who shared in his emphasis on service to God through song, dance, prayer, and joy of living. Calling him the *Baal Shem Tov* (Master of the Good Name), his following grew, particularly among the poorer, less well-educated elements of Polish Jewry. Crushed in the aftermath of the uprising of 1648, these people found a spiritual cause that allowed them to transcend the daily problems of life. Despite the antagonism of the rabbis and other opponents *(Mitnagdim),* the movement, known now as *Hassidism* (pietism), grew until it had won the hearts of masses of eastern European Jews. The *Mitnagdim* regarded the movement as a threat to the intellectual and religious integrity of Judaism. They particularly resented the *Hassidim* (pietists) for their deemphasis on study and, even more, for their elevation of the *Tzaddik* (righteous one), or leader among each group, to the position of a near-monarch. The position of the *Tzaddik* became hereditary, something of an innovation in Judaism, and the veneration of the *Tzaddik* struck the *Mitnagdim* as bordering on the worship

The practice of *Hassidism*
has continued to modern times.
These *Hassidim* are celebrating
Lag Beomer in Israel.

of humans. Gradually, as passions cooled, the groups reached something of a rapprochement, perhaps due to their common opposition to liberalizing tendencies within the Jewish community. The *Mitnagdim* began to recover a concern for the emotional needs of the individual, and the *Hassidim* laid greater stress on study of the texts of Judaism.

EMANCIPATION

During the seventeenth century, Jews quietly began to settle in England and parts of France. Their acceptance was based partly on respect accorded to the "Children of Israel," partly on economic self-interest. They began to engage in commerce and scholarship, helping to establish banks and promote international trade.

By the second half of the eighteenth century, more and more privileged Jews were exiting from Europe's ghettos. In some cases, they were allowed to enter the university and to live in a place of their choosing. Moses Mendelssohn (1729–1786) played a major role in abetting the integration of the Jew into western society. Having received a traditional Jewish education, he traveled from Dessau to Berlin. There, in addition to continuing his Jewish studies, he studied western subjects and became a close friend of Gotthold Ephraim Lessing, a Christian liberal and an outstanding playwright and thinker. Under the stimulation of this friendship, Mendelssohn developed a fine German writing style and won an award for an essay on philosophy.

Mendelssohn not only drew the attention of Berlin's liberal Christians but gained access to its literary circles. He believed that the Jews must participate in both Jewish and national (German) culture freely and knowledgeably. In order to help German Jews feel more at home in their host culture, he translated the Bible into German. From the Jewish viewpoint, Mendelssohn enabled Jews and Christians to gain in mutual appreciation. However, many young German Jews, including his own children, lost the desire to preserve their Jewish heritage. Seeking full acceptance into German society and refusing to limit themselves, they accepted baptism. (Felix Mendelssohn, his grandson, was baptized at infancy.)

Mendelssohn influenced the thinking of Europe's royalty. Stirred by humanitarian impulses and/or by a belief that, with civil rights, the Jews would ultimately abandon their unique status, Joseph II of Austria and other rulers gradually withdrew the social and economic restrictions that had been placed upon Jews for centuries. The ghetto walls began to totter; by the French Revolution, they collapsed.

The National Assembly of France in 1791 admitted French Jews to equal status. This phenomenon was repeated in 1796 in Holland, in 1798 in Italy, and by 1812 in Germany.

But there was a price. Summoned to an assembly in Paris by Emperor Napoleon in 1806, representatives of the French Jewish community were presented with a list of questions that could be reduced to one: "Are you a Frenchman first and a Jew second, or is the opposite true?" The representatives gave the expected answers. The price of civil rights was to be an end to Jewish communal distinctiveness and (perhaps unexpectedly) a great deal of assimilation.

The reaction following the defeat of Napoleon included a temporary reinstatement of some of the old prejudicial decrees against the Jews, but the process of integration and assimilation continued and was reinforced by the participation of Jews in the armies of the lands in which they lived. By the end of the nineteenth century, Jews were emancipated in all of the countries of western and central Europe.

RUSSIA

Originally barred from Russia for religious reasons, Jews were gradually absorbed by Russia as it expropriated the lands of its neighbors to the west. The czars took two approaches to the Jews in their empire: they restricted the residence and behavior of Jews as much as possible, and they encouraged Jews to convert to Christianity by offering privileges to the converts.

Between 1649 and 1881, approximately twelve hundred enactments were issued against the Jews by the government of Russia. A particularly damaging one in 1827 called for the conscription of Jews between the ages of twelve and forty-three. This meant that for much of life, Jews were unable to observe *Halakhah*.

Alexander II (emperor from 1855 to 1881) introduced some liberalization into Russia. Many of the decrees against the Jews were lifted. In 1881, he was assassinated and the reforms were ended. The infamous "Blood Libel" was revived and led to riots in several cities. The hand of the government was seen in these riots. The principal adviser to Czar Alexander III was quoted as saying that the "Jewish problem" would be solved by converting one-third of Russian Jews, allowing one-third to emigrate, and killing the rest. Pogroms became common. Laws excluded Jews from all villages and rural areas except in Poland. In 1891, they were also driven from large cities. In 1903, a pogrom destroyed a large number of Jews in Kishinev, Rumania. Three hundred such pogroms took place within that year in Russia

alone. In 1911, a Jewish worker, Mendel Beilis, was arrested and accused of the ritual murder of a Christian child. The trial ran for two years, accompanied by a government campaign of anti-Semitism. By the eve of World War I, Russian Jews were living in terrible social, economic, and political conditions. At the mercy of a government that despised them, restricted in every way, they were reliving the plight of their ancestors in central and western Europe in the Middle Ages.

ENLIGHTENMENT

In western Europe, following Mendelssohn, the movement known as *Haskalah* (enlightenment) had deeply touched the entire Jewish community. German Jewish scholars engaged in the *Wissenschaft* (science) of Judaism. Using tools of western scholarship, they researched the history and traditions of the Jews. Religious reform followed and accompanied the *Haskalah*. Efforts were made to recast Jewish religious worship in a mold of nineteenth-century German Protestantism. Instrumental music was introduced into the service. Hebrew was replaced by the vernacular as the primary language of worship. Men and women sat together. The head covering *(Kipah)* and prayer shawl *(Tallit)* were discarded. Some congregations substituted a Sunday service for the Jewish Sabbath worship.

The more traditional elements in each community reacted strongly to this radical reformation. Neo-Orthodox leaders like Samson Raphael Hirsch (1808–1888) were willing to accept the validity of western culture as a component in life as long as it did not challenge the validity of the *Halakhah*. Others like Moses Sofer (1762–1839) forbade their followers to even read the works of Moses Mendelssohn or to acquire a secular education. Extreme reformers like Samuel Holdheim (1806–1860) sought to define Judaism as a pure religion without ethnic or national components. Moderate reformers, the most important of whom was Zacharias Frankel (1801–1875), remained essentially faithful to Jewish tradition but accepted the need for modernization, insisting only that modernization proceed carefully and be controlled by the scholars who would maintain essential continuity with the past. Each of these positions survived its exponents and is represented in the American Jewish community today (see pp. 34–36).

A crowd demonstrating concern
for Soviet Jews.

In eastern Europe, the *Haskalah* (enlightenment) took a different course and initiated a secular form of Jewish culture. Calls for religious reform were muted. The Russian Jews did not wish to imitate the religious forms of their neighbor. A literature of nationalism appeared. After the reaction to the pogrom of 1881, Jews began to despair of integration into Russian life and to dream of national liberation. Leo Pinsker (1821–1891) wrote a pamphlet, "Auto-Emancipation," calling on Jews to recreate the Jewish homeland in Palestine. Others took up the idea. Many religious leaders, recalling the aftermath of the Sabbatean debacle, were cool to the idea. They preached patience until the coming of the Messiah. But with conditions deteriorating daily, many Jews were prepared to "stimulate" the messianic moment in history.

ZIONISM

The land of Israel had passed through the hands of many masters. Jewish settlement, continuous throughout the generations, waxed and waned according to political and economic conditions. Following the persecutions in Spain, many Jews migrated to the Holy Land. After 1492, this phenomenon of Spanish immigrants intensified. By the sixteenth century, a large group of mystics had settled in Safed, Tiberias, Hebron, and Jerusalem. Many of these settlers devoted themselves almost entirely to prayer and study, depending upon the contributions of Jews from around the world for their support. At the end of the nineteenth century, agricultural settlements were established by Russian Jews, supported by Baron Edmon Rothschild of the famous banking family. These settlers began to reclaim the desert and swamp that had resulted from centuries of neglect.

The beginnings of political Zionism can be traced to 1894, when Alfred Dreyfus, a French-Jewish captain, was tried for treason in France. Among the journalists attending the trial was Theodor Herzl (1860–1904), an assimilated Jew from Vienna. It was clear to Herzl and others that Dreyfus was being used as a scapegoat in order to divert attention from the miserable performance of the French army in the Franco-Prussian western lands. If Parisian crowds could shout "Down with the Jews," there was no hope for Jews living in the Diaspora.

Seized by this thought, Herzl quickly produced a small book, "The Jewish State," in which he argued that only in a national home would Jews find normalcy and safety. For the rest of his life Herzl devoted himself to this dream of a homeland for his people. He aroused the masses of Jews in Europe and the United States, though the most assimilated Jews were indifferent and, in some cases, hostile to his ideas. In 1897, the first of a series of Zionist conferences attracted representatives of Jewish communities around the world. Herzl was willing to consider Great Britain's offer to make Uganda the Jewish homeland, but he discovered that the ideas of a Jewish homeland and *Eretz Yisrael* (the land of Israel) were identical in the hearts and minds of Jews throughout the world. Herzl then focused his attention on obtaining a charter for a Jewish homeland in Palestine from the leading powers in the world. Exhausted by his efforts, he died at the age of forty-four.

The movement launched by Herzl grew and prospered. The Jewish National Fund, established by the Zionist Congress, gathered funds from world Jewry to drain swamps, plant trees, and purchase land in Palestine (most of it from absentee Arab landowners). A steady stream of Jews immigrated to Palestine throughout the early decades of the twentieth century.

But more than the resettlement of a people was at stake. It was in fact an entire culture that was being reborn. The immigrants insisted upon using Hebrew, the ancestral language hitherto used primarily for religious purposes. They wanted Hebrew to become the daily language of the *Yishuv* (the Jewish community in Palestine), thus signifying its direct link to the land and to their roots. Never before had an ancient language been successfully revived. Now, writers (some of whom had begun their work while in Russia as part of the *Haskalah* movement) and other talents produced poetry, fiction, drama, philosophy, art, and music as part of a renaissance of Jewish culture.

The *Yishuv* was innovative in other ways. A new form of agricultural settlement, the *Kibbutz* (collective), developed in Palestine. In the *Kibbutz,* men and women shared equally in the labor and in the profits of their labor. Having been denied access to the land for centuries, Jews developed a commitment to labor and to the land.

Prompted by Henrietta Szold (1860–1945), American founder of the Jewish women's Zionist organization known as *Hadassah,* work was begun which led to the eventual development of the finest hospital in the Middle East. The Hebrew University, first of the network of universities and technical institutions that were to rise in Palestine, was established in 1925. Palestine became a major center of Jewish life, attracting support and loyalty from all over the world. It was a unique historical phenomenon: the return of a people to its land and the revival of a national existence after a hiatus of two thousand years of Diaspora.

World War I (1914–1918) proved of crucial importance to the Jewish people. On the one hand, Jewish life in eastern Europe was seriously disrupted. On the other hand, while they fought loyally for the armies of their countries, Jews contributed significantly to the war effort of the Allies. After much delay, Jews were allowed to form a "Jewish legion" which fought in the British army, seeing action in Palestine against the Turks. In addition, Chaim Weizmann (1874–1952), a Russian-born scientist and Zionist leader living in England, was able to influence the British (into whose hands the League of Nations placed Palestine after the war) to issue the Balfour Declaration in 1917. This statement of official government policy said that Great Britain "viewed with favor, the establishment of a national home for the Jewish people in Palestine." At long last Herzl's idea of a charter had borne fruit. This announcement strengthened the Zionist cause considerably and encouraged more and more Diaspora Jews who were living in miserable conditions to make *Aliyah* (literally, "ascent," used to refer to settlement in Israel).

THE UNITED STATES

Jewish life in the United States began in 1654 when twenty-three Jews, fleeing the inquisition in Brazil, were granted permission to settle there, on the condition that they did not need public charity. In the eighteenth century, Jewish communities sprang up in such cities as Newport (where the oldest synagogue building in the United States is still in daily use), Philadelphia, Savannah, and Charleston.

Most of the earliest Jewish immigrants were *Sefardim,* descendants of the Spanish-Portuguese exiles of the fifteenth century. By 1802 there were *Ashkenazic* congregations (central-eastern European rite), and soon the *Ashkenazim* far outnumbered the *Sefardim.* The majority of Jews immigrating in the 1830s, 40s, and 50s were from central Europe, particularly Germany.

Many of the first rabbis who came to America were liberals, sympathetic to the ideals of Reform Judaism. With its emphasis on individual autonomy and its tendency to shed those aspects of Judaism which make the Jew outwardly distinctive, Reform Judaism proved attractive to many Jews. In 1824, a Reform temple was established in Charleston, South Carolina. Others arose all over the country in the following years.

In Rabbi Isaac Mayer Wise (1819–1900) the Reform movement found an organizing genius. Through his efforts, the Union of American Hebrew Congregations, the first congregational organization in America, was established in 1873. He also founded the first lasting rabbinical seminary, the Hebrew Union College, in 1875. Wise hoped to unify American Jewry through these institutions, but his hopes soon faded as he began to reflect the ideas of radical reformers. Other groups within the American Jewish community felt compelled to create their own institutions. To understand this, one must note that, beginning in the last two decades of the nineteenth century, America accepted millions of immigrants including significant numbers of eastern European Jews. These Jews settled in the largest cities of the country, mainly on the eastern seaboard.

The mass of eastern European Jews soon outnumbered the German Jews that had preceded them, just as the latter had outnumbered the *Sefardim* who had preceded them. Organizing a variety of cultural, social, and political groupings, the most recent arrivals remained relatively isolated from other American Jews and, like other immigrant groups, from other Americans. The German Jewish elite was concerned about the integration of the new immigrants into American life. It was clear that the new arrivals were not candidates for Reform Judaism. Therefore, several leaders, themselves Reform Jews, helped to establish a Conservative seminary—the Jewish Theological Seminary—in New York City in 1886. Actually, the Conservative position had been represented earlier by leaders such as Isaac Leeser (1806–1868), *Hazzan* (religious leader) of the *Sefardic* congregation Mikveh Israel in Philadelphia. Leeser produced an English translation of the Hebrew Bible, preached in English to his congregation, and stimulated the creation of many Jewish institutions in Philadelphia.

Sabato Morais, who succeeded Leeser as *Hazzan* at Mikveh Israel, served as the first president of the Jewish Theological Seminary. These men accepted the need for moderate reform and modernization of Judaism, but were repelled by the radicalism of the Reform movement. In 1902, Solomon Schechter, internationally famed as the discoverer of the Cairo Genizah and its ancient literary treasures, came to New York to head the seminary. Under Schechter, the United Synagogue of America, an organization of Conversative synagogues established in 1913, became a counterforce to the Reform institutions established by Wise.

But there was a third response to the challenge of American Jewish life, that of the Orthodox. Many of the new eastern European immigrants found even the moderate position of the Jewish Theological Seminary to be unacceptable. For them, the goal was the recreation of the great *Yeshivot* (academies) of eastern Europe on American soil. The first such institution—'Etz Hayyim of New York—was established in 1886. This *Yeshivah* was different from its European prototypes in that students engaged in secular studies along with intensive study of traditional texts. In 1928, Orthodox Jews founded a liberal arts college which eventually developed into Yeshivah University, a major center of Jewish and general study in New York City. This institution and others that subsequently developed represented the Orthodox position in America, a position that demanded strict adherence to tradition in general and to *Halakhah* in particular.

Jewish life in America has been characterized by involvement in a host of cultural, social, fraternal, and religious organizations. From tiny local groups to national and international organizations, Jews worked to provide for the needs of others in America, Israel, and throughout the Diaspora. American Jews also developed a creative way of fulfilling the *Mitzvah* (commandment) of *Tzedakah* (philanthropy). *B'nai B'rith*, the largest social and philanthropic American-Jewish organization in the country, was founded in 1843. Beginning in Boston in 1895, Jewish communities began to merge their fundraising efforts into what came to be known as the Federation of Welfare Fund. Gradually, the Federation expanded its activities beyond coordinated fund raising. Today, the Federation is charged with the responsibility of community planning. It even publishes newspapers and journals that keep the members of the Jewish community informed of its activities.

This system of organization was put to the test following World War I, when many European Jews found themselves in precarious straits. With the Balfour Declaration and the various *Aliyot* (waves of immigration) to Palestine, American Jews began to take a major responsibility for meeting the needs of Jews around the world. All of this prepared them to meet the twin challenges of the crucial events in modern Jewish history: the Holocaust and the rebirth of the State of Israel.

THE HOLOCAUST

Before dealing with the Holocaust, a brief discussion of anti-Semitism is in order.

The Jewish people have experienced persecution and hostility for a major portion of their history. One of the more obvious reasons for anti-Semitism stems from differences in religious beliefs. Anti-Semitism was a recurrent phenomenon of Greek and Roman life. Regarding any deviants from the state religion as barbarians, Greek and Roman writers, dramatists, and rhetoricians accused the Jews of being inhumane, lazy, and superstitious. Fortunately, this literary anti-Semitism did not, as a rule, lead to violence against the Jews. Nevertheless,

Greek and Roman writers may be seen as the originators of anti-Semitism, for they singled out the Jews as being different from their neighbors and a threat to the established order.

Anti-Semitism may also have a psychological base. People sometimes imagine that a certain person or group is an enemy, to be hated, feared, and possibly harmed. If a person feels dissatisfied with life or is frustrated by events, it is tempting to seek a scapegoat—someone or some group that can be blamed for the problems. Group hatred, then, is a function, in part, of psychological distress. Jews have felt the sting of this hatred, particularly during periods of economic, social, or political stress within the lands in which they lived.

There have been times in Jewish history when hatred of the Jews was related to the poverty of those who hated them. Sometimes, Jews were restricted to certain occupations or denied the right to own land in order to prevent them from achieving economic success.

Xenophobia, or fear of the stranger, provides yet another source of anti-Semitism. The foreigner is often seen as inferior, as someone to be mistrusted, feared, and even hated. Without a home of their own, the Jews of the Diaspora have had few alternatives to suffering the barbs of their enemies in each host country.

With this background, we now proceed to examine the events of the Holocaust, the blackest chapter in all of Jewish history.

In 1923, Adolf Hitler founded the National Socialist party in Germany. Broken in spirit and economically depressed as a result of World War I, the Germans saw Hitler as a man who could restore national pride and financial stability. Hitler convinced many Germans that their problems were caused by the Communists, the Socialists, and, above all, the Jews. Quickly gaining dictatorial power, he was in a position to act upon the racial theories that he expounded. He claimed that the "Aryan" (Teutonic) races were the elite of humanity; the Jews, the scum of the earth. He circulated the "Protocols of the Elders of Zion," a ridiculous forgery that purported to be the minutes of a secret meeting at which leaders of world Jewry had plotted to gain control of the world. Building upon centuries of prejudice against Jews fomented by church and state, Hitler was able to release wild, beastly anger against the Jews of Germany. In 1933, a national boycott of Jewish-owned stores was followed by a civil service law that barred Jews from public office and from posts at the universities and other cultural institutions. At this point many Jewish intellectuals such as Albert Einstein began to leave the country; but most Jews, deeply attached to their country, remained. The latter were convinced that a highly cultured land such as Germany would not permit such measures to continue very long. But conditions became worse. There were public burnings of books by Jews, and Jewish children were segregated from others at school. In 1935, Jews were declared to be ineligible for citizenship and the universities were closed to them. In 1938, the government took possession of all money owned by Jews in excess of two thousand dollars. That year also brought the infamous *Kristelnacht,* in which, during one night, every synagogue in the country was attacked and burned while countless Jewish men, women, and children were beaten. The Nazi attitude was summarized by Joseph Goebbels, propagandist for the government:

> A Jew is for me an object of physical disgust. I vomit when I
> see one. . . . Christ cannot possibly have been a Jew. . . .

Goebbels and others formulated a rationale for the atrocities, claiming that the elimination or subjugation of non-Aryan races was a moral necessity in order to cleanse the land. Shamefully, professors and other cultural figures approved of this "Racial Science." Between 1933 and 1935, sixty thousand Jews left Germany. By 1939, two hundred thousand had gone, helped by the philanthropy of fellow Jews in America and other free countries. After 1939, when Hitler invaded Poland and World War II began, the doors of Germany slammed shut and those remaining found themselves trapped and doomed to experience the greatest nightmare in Jewish and world history.

Though the invasion of Poland brought England and France into the war, Hitler's armies soon overran Norway, Denmark, and the low countries of western Europe. In 1940, Hitler invaded Russia. He viewed the Slavs as being almost as low on the ladder of humanity as the Jews. Heinrich Himmler, head of the S.S. (Schutzstaffel, military and police unit of the Nazi Party), summed up this attitude as follows:

> What happens to a Russian or a Czeck does not interest me in
> the slightest. . . . Whether nations live in prosperity or starve to
> death interests me only to the extent that we need them as slaves
> for our culture.

This contempt for the non-Aryan races led to the slaughter of fifteen million Russians, two million Poles, two million Greeks and Yugoslavs, and two hundred thousand Gypsies, all in the name of "Anti-Partisan welfare."

A statue at *Yad Vashem,*
a monument dedicated
to the six million Jews
who perished in the Holocaust.

The "Jewish problem" was placed in the hands of Reinhard Heydrich, Gestapo chief, and a major named Adolf Eichmann. In 1939, Jews were deported from Germany. In Poland, they were moved from rural areas to restricted areas of the cities—a twentieth-century recreation of the medieval ghetto. In the process, many died of starvation and disease. Now, the Nazis sought a "final solution" to the Jewish problem. Death camps were set up in Auschwitz, Buchenwald, Dachau, Treblinka, and other places. Crowded into cattle cars, Jews were transported to these camps for "resettlement." Some died en route. Upon arrival, all but the strongest (required for work) were put to death. In the early years, this was done by shooting; later a more efficient form of execution was invented. Those slated to die were taken for "showers." However, instead of emitting water, these showers emitted an asphyxiating gas. After killing Jews in this manner, the S.S. men would enter the area and remove anything of value—rings, gold teeth, hair. The leading scientific community of Europe had found a way of raising murder to the level of a science; for with this method, they could put to death seven thousand people a day in each camp.

In 1941, the United States entered the war. Gradually the tide of the war changed. This reversal was not, however, permitted to interfere with the "holy task" of exterminating the Jews. At one point, when trains were desperately needed to transport soldiers to the battlefront, Eichmann refused to release them. Nothing was permitted to interfere with the "final solution."

Nazi propaganda ingeniously hid the truth of the death camps for a long time. Gradually, as Jews began to realize what these camps meant, resistance developed. The most famous example of this resistance took place in the Warsaw ghetto where, in 1942, forty thousand Jews armed with small arms and bottles of gasoline fought the tanks, airplanes, and cannon of the Germans for thirty-three days.

In 1944, with the Nazi situation approaching desperation, Eichmann contacted representatives of the Hungarian Jewish community with an amazing offer. He would spare the lives of one million Jews in return for trucks, soap, coffee, and other materials. The offer was transmitted to the west and, in a short time, pledges were received to guarantee the money. One problem remained—where to send the Jews. Eichmann had said that they could go anywhere but to Palestine. Hitler, it seemed, had promised his friend, the mufti (Muslim judge) of Jerusalem, that Jews would not be permitted to settle in the Holy Land.

The deal collapsed because no country would accept all or part of the Jews. It was a dramatic incident but not an isolated one. In the course of the early years of Hitler's rule, some Jews had escaped Germany on ships and traveled from port to port only to discover that they would not be permitted to land. Some of these ships broke open in the sea; others were forced to return to Germany where their passengers were taken off the ships and sent to the death camps. Leaders of the Jewish community begged the Allies to bomb the railroad tracks leading to the death camps or even the camps themselves; the request was refused because "it would detract from the war effort."

It is not easy to explain all of this. Germany, the world leader of culture, unleashed the greatest barbarism in Jewish and world history. Most leading intellectual and religious leaders and heads of government around the world were either silent on the issue or supported the German government and its program.

Here and there, individuals and groups defied the Nazis. King Christian of Denmark saved all of Danish Jewry in a daring act of heroism. Today in Israel, next to the national monument to Holocaust victims—*Yad Vashem*—there is a small garden in which each tree honors an individual or a group that saved Jews from Hitler.

THE STATE OF ISRAEL

In 1945 the war came to an end. The facts of the Holocaust became known: one out of every three Jews living before the war was dead. The remnant of European Jewry was living in concentration camps, now renamed "displaced persons camps" by the Allies. The survivors were unwilling to return to their homes. Most wanted to go to Palestine or America. In 1939, Britain had drastically limited Jewish immigration to the Holy Land. During the war, Palestinian Jews had put aside their anger prompted by Britain's actions. Now, with the war ended, acute pain and shame over the facts of the Holocaust galvanized Palestinian and world Jewry. Jews who had previously been cool or hostile to Zionism joined in a united effort to save the displaced persons and to gain entrance for them into Palestine. In Palestine itself, the immigration issue became critical. Jews and Arabs began to quarrel, and the movement began, albeit illegally, to transport European Jews to the Holy Land.

In 1942, Jewish leaders from around the world had gathered in New York to call for an opening of the gates of Palestine. They specifically called for a partition of the land into Jewish and Arab states. After the war, the first Zionist conference endorsed this position. Tensions built in Palestine. The Jews demanded a renewal of immigration, while the Arabs were cool or opposed. Britain was caught between its commitment to the Balfour Declaration and its concern for Arab-British relations. As tensions mounted, the British turned the issue over to the newly created United Nations. In a rare moment of unanimity between the United States and the Soviet Union, each acting from a combination of humanitarian and political motivations, the United Nations on November 29, 1947, voted to partition Palestine. The Zionists embraced the proposal, while the Arabs threatened to abort it.

Britain was not happy with the decision, which, it felt, placed obstacles in the way of the transfer of power. By the end of 1947, Arab bands were attacking Jewish settlements. Although the latter were usually able to defend themselves, they were often disarmed and jailed. Quietly, the *Yishuv* created a government in waiting headed by David Ben-Gurion, chairman of the Jewish Agency, the organization of the *Yishuv*. The British worked against the transition by disrupting vital services, such as the postal service and the railroad. The new state would begin life without a treasury or taxing authority. Arab guerrilla bands from outside Palestine were already attacking Jewish settlements. Time was running out. On May 14, 1948 (the fifth of Iyar on the Jewish calendar), David Ben-Gurion and his new cabinet proclaimed the independence of the State of Israel.

Israel today is the only democracy in the Middle East. Its presidents from Chaim Weizmann on have been elected by the Knesset, or parliament. The prime minister, as in England, is the leader of the party in power. A free press exists, and free public education is offered to all Israeli citizens. Israel has become a center of education, medicine, scientific research, and cultural achievement. Refugees and immigrants from lands of persecution like the Soviet Union and Iraq, as well as from all over the free world, have been accepted. Israel is a source of tremendous pride for Jews all over the world who see in it a refuge for Jews in distress and a bastion of democracy in the Middle East.

Ideas and Ideals

Many religions have a highly developed set of creeds or dogmas that a believer is required to affirm if he or she wishes to be part of that religion. Judaism took a different path. What binds Jews to each other are, in the main, common traditions, ceremonies, language, prayers, and a broad range of concepts. This does not mean that Judaism lacks distinctive beliefs about human nature or the good life; it means that these beliefs are usually indeterminate—that they are not precisely defined. Thus there is considerable latitude for an individual to interpret the beliefs according to his or her own conscience. Part II examines some of the ideas that have played a key role in Jewish history and Jewish belief.

As previously indicated, the idea of *Berit,* or covenant, has always been central in Judaism. The act of circumcision *(Berit Milah)* is the formal ceremony by which a male baby enters the Jewish community. The concept of covenant finds expression in three other concepts: God, Israel, and Torah. God and Israel are the covenanters; the Torah is the link between them. God is seen as the giver of the Torah, and Israel as the receiver. These three concepts are closely related, and this relationship is pointed up in the folk saying "Israel, God, and Torah are one."[1]

If we develop the implications of this statement, we will come to grasp the structure and character of Judaism. This inquiry into Judaism could begin with any of these concepts. Some would argue that it should begin with Israel. Their argument would go like this:

The people of Israel produced their own concept of God as well as their own Torah. When people write, they reflect their own experi-

ences and values. The Jews, as a result of their experiences, developed institutions, laws, goals, and models of behavior. They formulated ideas about the universe, the role of God in that universe, human nature, the good life, and the role of the Jewish people in history. These ideas, together with laws, customs, rituals, and traditions, were incorporated into the sacred literature, which serves as a mirror of Jewish collective thinking.

Others would start with God. They would formulate their argument in words like these:

God existed before creation of the world. For reasons of His own (and Jews did speculate as to these reasons), God chose Israel to be His people, gave them the Torah, and entered into the Berit *with them.*

Finally, others would say that any examination of Judaism ought to begin with the Torah. Their argument would be as follows:

Israel became God's people through its acceptance of the Torah. God and His expectations of people can be known through the study of the Torah.

It is important to realize that these views are in fundamental agreement on a number of points while they differ on others. They agree that Jews find fulfillment through the study and implementation of the ideas and ideals of the Torah. They agree that God is the model whose traits of love, kindness, justice, and so on, are to be imitated. They disagree in that, of the three views, the latter two see the ideals as coming to people from the outside. They receive the Torah and learn to understand it and live according to its teachings. The first view, the one beginning with Israel, sees people erecting the ideals and projecting them outward.

The following sections incorporate some of the most important passages from classical Jewish literature dealing with human beings and their nature, the relationship of people and society, and the concept of God. A study of these sources indicates that many of the differences that separate the traditionalist and the modernist today are the same differences that separated the traditionalist and the modernist of the early years of the Common Era.

HUMAN BEINGS AND THEIR NATURE

In discussing the ideals of any civilization, it is probably best to begin with an examination of the way in which that civilization thinks of the individual. Actually, the way in which a society views the nature, character, and potentialities of an individual as well as the individual's relationship to others is the best indication of the views of that society toward the entire group. In fact, it may well be that what really differentiates one society from another is the way in which it thinks about the individual.

When thinkers approach the subject of human beings, they usually begin from one of two points of view. Either they start from an ideal of what people should be, or they start from a more practical vantage point describing people as they are. In rabbinic thought, both approaches are found. The rabbis never tired of projecting the ideals they felt to be appropriate; yet, at the same time, they recognized the accomplishments and failings of people. Their idealism was not naiveté; rather it was an expression of optimism based on past experience and a belief in future growth and improvement. They taught that people were commanded by God to fulfill their potentialities as human beings. The rabbis believed this could be accomplished if people applied the principles of the Torah in daily life situations.

In Judaism, human beings are seen as being created with two basic impulses, one good and the other evil. This does not mean that the two must always be in conflict. Rather, one can be seen as representing those aspects of one's personality that have to do with reason and purpose or choice; the other can be seen as relating essentially to desire or raw energy. It is true, according to the rabbis, that these impulses often conflict. But if the evil impulse is harnessed properly, it may well serve good purposes. Thus, for example, ambition may lead one person to steal and another to heal. Anger may cause one human being to behave irrationally and another to fight evil. The sex drive may cause one man to rape and another to marry and raise a family. In fact, the rabbis said, were it not for the evil impulse, no one would ever marry, have children, build a house, or plant a vineyard.[2] As usual, the emphasis is on the ability to choose. Here the rabbis seized on a biblical verse for support: "Sin crouches at the door, its urge is toward you yet you can be its master" (Genesis 4:7).

The early stories of Genesis represent the foundations or proof texts for this major rabbinic response to the problem of evil. Noting God's warning to Adam and to Cain, the rabbis decided that evil is a by-product of the human ability to choose. In fact, said the rabbis, this ability is the really distinctive characteristic of humans. To eliminate the possibility of evil by eliminating the human ability to choose (wrongly) would mean to put an end to human existence as we know it. Without choice there is no responsibility, no meaningful human existence. Thus the entire system of rabbinic thinking is based on the principle that people have the freedom of moral choice and that it is in their power to direct and control their actions. The rabbis admitted that

much of a person's life is determined before he or she is born or shortly afterward. Yet, they have never surrendered the idea of moral choice. A legend relates:

> Before the formation of the fetus in the mother's womb, the Holy One, Blessed be He, decrees whether he shall be male or female, weak or strong, rich or poor, short or tall, ugly or handsome, fat or thin, despised or proud, etc. But whether he will be righteous or wicked is not decreed, for this God gives over into man's hands.[3]

What did the rabbis do about the theological problem of human freedom versus God's omniscience? They did not try to solve it but rather admitted the truth of both, apparently contradictory, principles. "Everything is foreseen by God, but freedom of choice is given to man"[4] or "everything is in the hand of Heaven except for the fear of Heaven,"[5] which can be paraphrased as "God can do anything except make man religious." They maintained human choice and thus held people responsible for their actions, while, at the same time, asserting that God is all knowing and all powerful.

The rabbis took the matter of human responsibility very seriously. They saw people in the role of God's partner, charged with the responsibility of taking care of the world and moving it toward perfection. They also would not accept the idea that heredity excuses one's moral failings. Why, it may be asked, were all things created in great number—for example, trees, plants, animals, birds—except for humankind? The answer is that humans were created singly so that the wicked cannot blame their wickedness on their ancestors. If the wicked say, "It is because of my ancestors who were wicked that I am evil today," the righteous can respond, "Your excuse is not valid. We both stem from the same parentage."[6]

Sometimes a person has good intentions and makes a mistake, perhaps a serious one. Sometimes a person does the right thing for the wrong reason. This raises the question: Which is more important in judging a person's behavior, act or intention? In Judaism, the answer depends on the situation. If we are dealing with relationships among people, then it is the act by which a person is judged and intent is of secondary importance. If we ask the same question in regard to an individual's relationship to God, Judaism responds that it is the intent by

The velvet mantles covering these Torah scrolls are richly decorated. The metal pointer, or *yad,* on the open scroll is used to help the reader keep his place without actually touching the scroll.

47

which he or she is judged and the act is of secondary importance. This explains why commandments in Judaism are usually divided into two categories: those between an individual and God and those between one person and another.

Another question that all philosophies and religions grapple with is that of the essential nature of human beings. The rabbis knew that people are physical beings, but they also believed that there is more to people than their physical nature. This "more" they designated as soul. Yet, though they saw the physical nature of people as different from the "heavenly" nature, they insisted that there is an essential unity to people—that they are unified beings.

This idea becomes important when one considers the question of evil. Many religions associate all that is evil or base in humans with the human body and bodily needs. These religions usually decide that people cannot achieve their full spiritual growth unless they are prepared to neglect or even suppress the needs or desires of their body. Judaism took a different path. It decreed that a person is obligated to take care of his or her body; to consult a doctor if ill; even to enjoy food, drink, and sexual pleasure (within marriage) as part of a normal life. This attitude is reflected in the following prayer which religious Jews recite every day.

> Blessed are You, O Lord our God, King of the universe, Who has formed man in wisdom and created within him many openings and tubes. You know that if one of these were to open or one of these were to be stopped up, it would be impossible to exist and to stand before You. Blessed are You, O Lord, Who heals all flesh and does wonderously.[7]

A typical talmudic story makes the same point. It concerns the famous teacher Hillel. Once, upon finishing his class at the academy, Hillel started to leave and was asked by his students about his destination. "I'm going to fulfill a *Mitzvah* (commandment)," he replied. They were intrigued and decided to follow him. To their surprise, he went to the public bath house. "What *Mitzvah*," they asked, "are you going to perform there?" "To bathe my body," he replied. "God has given me a soul which is pure and is to be kept in this state, so too He has given me a body, the house of the soul, which must be kept in the same condition."[8]

The unity of the body and soul and the Jewish belief that the body is not responsible for evil are further captured in this talmudic tale:

> Once there was a king who had a magnificent orchard with all types of fruit-bearing trees. Before embarking on a journey, he called two servants together and instructed them to take care of

the orchard and to guard it from thieves. He warned that they would be held responsible for any damage or loss to the orchard. These two servants were infirm; one was blind and the other lame. On the king's return he discovered that the fruit had all disappeared. He confronted the two servants: "What happened to the fruit?" he demanded. The blind man said, "I saw nothing." The lame man replied, "Surely you can't hold me responsible. I could never have climbed the trees even if I had wanted to steal the fruit." The king was not a fool. He knew what had happened. He placed the lame man on the shoulders of the blind man and said, "Thus you stole, as one man; so shall you be punished, as one man!"[9]

The rabbis applied this parable to the human body and soul, saying that when a person stands before God to be judged and his or her sins are recalled, the soul argues that it is blameless and that the body should be blamed, for only the body has the capacity to sin. The body responds that it is merely a physical mass incapable of action without a force —the soul—to direct it. The rabbis further maintained that God responds as did the king in the parable—that the body and the soul are inseparable, and together they act and must take responsibility for their actions.

The rabbis accepted the idea of an afterlife but never minimized the importance of the world in which we live. They taught that one ought to enjoy the pleasure of this world, as long as this enjoyment does not violate the moral law of the Torah. The ascetic is not the hero. "Wine does gladden the heart of man," says the Psalmist. Jewish holidays, particularly the Sabbath, are marked by the enjoyment of sensory pleasures. Of course, the Bible does relate instances of asceticism. In all ages, there have been those people whose religious faith led them to want to give up normal pleasures. In the Torah, such an individual is known as a Nazarite. The Nazarite voluntarily vows to abstain from some physical pleasure, generally the drinking of wine. The rabbis could not abolish such a tradition, considering its source, but they did not hesitate to show their disapproval of it. They pointed out that, upon completion of the term of his vow, the Nazarite was required to appear in the Temple in Jerusalem and to bring a sacrifice—a sin offering! The rabbis declared that this sin offering was required because, in a sense, the Nazarite had sinned against himself by denying himself what is permitted. And, they concluded, if one who denies himself wine is called a sinner, how much more so one who lives a life of complete asceticism.

There is an important corollary to this approach to the enjoyment of the pleasures of life. In Judaism, poverty is not considered a virtue, nor a desired state; and riches are not, in themselves, seen as being sinful. On the contrary, people who acquire riches through honest means are considered fortunate. Moreover, they are seen as being worthy of praise if they share their riches with others. This issue of poverty needs to be understood. Judaism believes that each person is unique and that each person is capable of contributing something unique to the world. If people are poor, they may lose their self-respect and may have to employ all of their energies in supplying their basic needs. This situation may well rob them of the opportunity to develop their own special talents and capacities, and thus result in their being spiritually impoverished. It also robs the entire community of the benefits of what they have to offer. Thus, the removal of poverty is seen as a responsibility of the entire community. The Jewish community has been particularly successful in fulfilling the *Mitzvah* of *Tzedakah,* or care of the needy. This commandment reflects the religious obligation to offer help to those who have fallen and to lift them up.

As a result of their views of the nature of human nature, Jews have a rather positive attitude toward the physical dimension of life. This does not mean that from time to time there were not some Jews who did encourage an ascetic approach to life (such Jews did appear throughout history), but it is possible to say that in the mainstream of Jewish thought their ideas did not prevail and one can be a thoroughly observant and pious Jew without giving up the basic pleasures of the world.

PEOPLE AND SOCIETY

Rabbinic Judaism both recognizes and emphasizes the fact that people are social creatures and fulfill themselves as part of society. Since this is true, it follows that people are obligated to contribute to the society—to take part in the life of the group. Two thousand years ago Hillel expressed the same attitude when he said, "Do not separate yourself from the community." Judaism teaches that a person's actions affect everyone around him. This point is illustrated by the following story.

> A man was traveling by boat in the company of others. He took a drill and began to bore a hole in the bottom of the ship. The others said, "What are you doing?" He replied, "It's my own business and none of yours. I am making a hole under my own seat!"[10]

Judaism stresses the relationship of one person to another. The following rabbinic statement gives voice to this sense of interdependence.

How much labor must Adam have expended before he had bread to eat. He ploughed, sowed, reaped, piled up the sheaves, threshed, winnowed, selected the ears, sifted the flour, kneaded and baked and only after all of this, he ate; whereas I arise in the morning and find all this ready for me. And how much labor must Adam have expended before he obtained a garment to wear. He had to shear, wash the wool, comb and spin and weave and only after all of this obtain a garment to wear, whereas I get up in the morning and find all this ready for me. All the artisans attend and come to the door of my house and I get up and find all these things before me.[11]

Social approval was a major force in Jewish society. It was through this force that ideas and ideals affected the life of the individual. So important was public opinion in the minds of the rabbis that they almost equated it with divine favor: "He who earns the love of his fellow creatures earns the love of God; he who does not earn the love of his fellow creatures does not earn the love of God"[12] (a saying found among other peoples).

But rabbinic Judaism saw people as more than members of a group. It also stressed that individuals must make decisions and be responsible for their actions. Both roles are reflected in this rabbinic statement: "Which is the right course that a man should choose for himself? That which does honor to him who does it and which brings him honor from mankind."[13]

Underpinning this double awareness of people as individuals and as a part of society is the basic Jewish view that people are "created in the image of God." This view leads naturally to the expectation that people will live in a way that is worthy of their status. Among other things this means recognizing that one's fellow human beings are also "created in the image of God," and therefore an offense against another person is, in effect, an offense against God. Rabbi Akiba, commenting on Leviticus 19:18 ("You shall love your neighbor as yourself") said, "Do not say 'since I am despised, let my neighbor be despised with me.'" Rabbi Tanhuma added, "If you act in this manner, know who it is that you despise for in the image of God, He made man."[14]

This appreciation for self-esteem and esteem for others must ultimately lead to an examination of priorities. The rabbis were almost unanimous in stating that a person's first priority is to himself or herself. They accepted this as a legitimate part of human nature. But if people are preoccupied with their own needs, they cannot be completely fulfilled as human beings. Thus the rabbis also expected people to be concerned with the needs of others. Hillel expressed this idea in the following somewhat puzzling statement: "If I am not for myself, who will be for me? But if I am only for myself, what am I? And if not now, when?"[15]

The natural extension of this sense of self-concern is to be found in rabbinic discussion of preservation of life. The rabbis pointed to the legitimacy of self-defense: "He who rises up to slay you, rise up and slay him first."[16] There is no sense of "turning the other cheek" in this approach, but Jewish law does impose limitations that apply to the preservation of life in situations where a Jew must choose between violating a commandment in the Torah or losing his life. Of the 613 commandments in the Torah, 610 of them may be broken in order to save one's life. But there are three which may never be broken, even to preserve life. They are murder, sexual immorality, and idolatry.

A further limitation of the right to take life is exemplified in the following citations from rabbinic literature.

> A man came to a rabbi and said, "The ruler of my town has commanded me to murder a certain man or he will murder me. What shall I do?" The rabbi replied, "Let him kill you; do not commit murder. Why should you think that your blood is redder than his?"[17]

> Ulla ben Kosheb was sought by the [Roman] government. He fled and took refuge in Lud with Rabbi Joshua ben Levi. The officers of the government came and told the inhabitants of Lud that the entire city would be destroyed unless he was handed over. Rabbi Joshua came and convinced Ulla that he should let himself be handed over. Now Elijah, the prophet, was in the habit of appearing to Rabbi Joshua, but he came to him no more. Then Rabbi Joshua fasted many days and at last Elijah appeared. He said to Rabbi Joshua, "Should I reveal myself to informers?" "I did but act according to a teaching," said Rabbi Joshua. "Is that a proper teaching for the pious?" answered Elijah.[18]

THE CONCEPT OF GOD

As pointed out at the beginning of Part II, the lack of precision in defining Jewish belief affords Jews considerable freedom in establishing their own theology. This is clearly seen in regard to Jewish statements about God. First of all, Jewish theology is rather practical; it deals with God in relationship to people and their concerns. The rabbis were not interested in abstract speculation about God. For example, they would not ask such questions as "Can God create a stone so large that he himself cannot move it?" This question would be of interest to one who wishes to define the exact limits of God's power. It did not interest the rabbis because it seemed to be rather far from the daily practical concerns of life.

To know something of rabbinic theology, it is advisable to examine the *Aggadah:* "If one wishes to know God, let him study the *Aggadah.*" We first discover that for the Jew, the existence of God is an axiom—a truth that need not be demonstrated. Nowhere in the Bible nor in the early rabbinic literature do we find an attempt by a Jew to prove the existence of God to another Jew. This was an accepted truth that need not be questioned nor proven. It must, however, be remembered that in the ancient world only the Jews had a concept of an unseen God. The rabbis faced challenges from pagan thinkers on this matter and they had to defend their beliefs. Their responses were rather simple and not particularly convincing. Only in the post-talmudic age (after the seventh century), when the Jews came into contact with disciplined Muslim philosophers, did they begin to establish systematic philosophical systems which included "proofs" for the existence of God.

To see how how far the rabbis of the talmudic period were from such systematic theology, we need only return to the *Aggadah.* Here we are told that it was the patriarch Abraham who was the first to become aware of the one God and of the ethical demands which He makes on those who believe in Him. The Bible does not even provide a hint as to how Abraham came upon this revelation. The *Aggadah* offers the following speculations.

> Nimrod the king was warned by his astrologers that a child who would ultimately depose him was about to be born. They advised him to have the child killed. When the child [Abraham] was born, his father, Terah, hid him in a cave for three years with a nurse. When the child came out, he wanted to know which of the heavenly bodies was God. First he noticed the moon which lit up the darkness. "Ah," he said, "the stars must be the courtiers of the moon. This is my god," he proclaimed, and all through the night he worshipped it. But when the dawn came, the light of the sun shut out the light of the moon and the light of the stars. He cried out, "The light of the moon must be derived from the greater light of the sun," whereupon he worshipped the sun throughout the entire day. In the evening, when the sun set and the moon, stars, and planets rose, he realized, "Surely all of these have but one master, God."[19]
>
> When Abraham rejected the idolatry of his native city, his father brought him before Nimrod who demanded that he worship fire instead of the idols. Abraham said, "We would rather worship water which extinguishes the fire." Nimrod said, "Worship the water." Then Abraham said, "If so, we should worship

the cloud which contains the water." Nimrod said, "Worship the cloud." Abraham responded, "If so, we should worship the wind which scatters the clouds." Nimrod said, "Then worship the wind." And Abraham responded, "We should then worship man who contains the wind in his body."[20]

And the conclusion is to worship the one who is the ultimate Creator.

When talking of God, Jewish theology has always stressed the ideas of oneness or unity. In fact, the most famous verse in the Jewish religion, known to many Jews from the time of early childhood, says: "Hear, O Israel, the Lord is our God, the Lord is One" (Deuteronomy 6:4). This verse is the seed of many ideas: If God is one, then—

1. the world that He created is a unity;
2. all creatures are related (the children of one father are brothers and sisters);
3. all of nature is interrelated and interdependent;
4. the laws in nature are dependable;
5. there are standards of right and wrong, of laws and morals that have absolute validity.

Another basic Jewish belief about God is that He is free to act with purpose both in creation and in the conduct of the world. Judaism sees God as ever active, involved in history. There are other views that talk of a God who creates and then withdraws from the world. Judaism does not take this approach. Rather, it sees God as deeply interested in the world. The rabbis said that everything that was created was created for a purpose. "Despise not any man nor regard anything as impossible, for you find that there is no man who does not have his hour and no thing that does not have its place."[21]

This idea is illustrated in several legends about King David.

Once David said to God, "The world is good and beautiful with the one exception of insanity. What use is there to the world of the madman who runs about, tears his clothing, and is ridiculed and chased by little children?" God replied, "The time will come when you will beg me to afflict you with madness." Now when David fled from King Saul, he came to the city of Gath. The king of that city was Achish and his guards were the brothers of Goliath, who was slain by David. They demanded that David be put to death.

An ancient well, known as Abraham's Well, near Beersheba. Bedouins believe this well was used by Abraham.

Achish, although a heathen, was a moral man and tried to pacify them. In his distress David begged God to let him appear to be a madman before Achish and his court, and God granted his wish. Since the wife and daughter of Achish were both insane, we can understand the king's question: "Do I lack madness that you have brought this one to play the madman before me?" (I Samuel 21:15–16). So David was rescued, whereupon he said, "I will bless the Lord at all times" (see Psalm 34:1–2).[22]

On another occasion, David criticized God for having created a creature as useless as the spider.

> "They do nothing," said David, "but spin a web which is value-less." However, on one occasion, he hid and took refuge in a cave while Saul and his men were pursuing him. They were about to enter the cave and discover him, which would have meant certain death. But God sent a spider to weave a web across the opening, and Saul was convinced that David could not be in the cave since the web was unbroken.[23]

Finally, David complained that in addition to the spider, there is another useless creature—the wasp.

> Once, David came upon Saul and his men while they were sleeping in their camp. David intended to take something in order to show them that he could have killed the king but had not done so. As David was leaving the camp, Abner, Saul's general, stretched out his leg over the creeping David and pinned him down. David escaped from this dangerous situation only when a wasp stung Abner, causing him to move his leg and thus free David.[24]

While stressing the idea of order and purpose in creation, the rabbis were aware that the Bible speaks of miracles. They were not prepared to say that God lacks power to perform wonders, yet they were committed to the idea that the world is orderly, and tried to explain the miraculous within the framework of this order. One way they did this was to say that ten wonderful things were created on the eve of the first Sabbath (for example, the rod of Moses, the manna). By including these miraculous things within creation, the rabbis were trying to make them part of the plan of an orderly universe.

Another idea that has played an important role in Judaism is the concept that God is totally spiritual—that He has no body and no physical characteristics. The Bible as well as rabbinic literature contains many descriptions of God that speak of physical form and human emotions and reactions. To explain this fact, the rabbis pointed out that we are forced to use human terms and apply them to God. "We borrow terms for His creatures to apply to Him in order to help our understanding." "The Torah speaks according to the language of the sons of man."[25]

In trying to make the concept of God meaningful, the rabbis used some strong anthropomorphic and anthropopathic descriptions. The first of these terms means speaking of God as if He had human characteristics. The second means speaking of God as if He had human feelings. Sometimes the *Aggadah* uses descriptions that are so earthy that they seem almost disrespectful. But the rabbis did not see it that way. They believed that God and humans can have a direct personal relationship despite the fact that the former is totally spiritual and the latter only partially so.

Several good examples of this are found in the *Aggadah*. For example, we are told that God acted as "best man" at the marriage of Adam and Eve and that he helped the bride braid her hair in order to make her attractive to her husband. In another passage we are told that God visited Abraham when the latter was recovering from his circumcision operation. We are also told that God consoled Jacob when the latter had a loss and that He buried Moses. Notice that God is here described as actually performing those acts that are presented as commandments for humankind to observe: caring for the fatherless bride, visiting the sick, comforting the mourners, and burying the dead. These passages are illustrations of the imitation of God, the leading principle of rabbinic ethics. People are commanded to imitate God who treats His creatures with love and compassion.

Another attribute of God that is stressed is His omnipresence. This is a practical matter for it means that wherever a person may be, he or she stands in the presence of God. This is intended to impress upon people the necessity of acting as human beings should at all times and in all places. That this sense of God's omnipresence is not easy to achieve is illustrated in the following story.

> Rabbi Yohanan ben Zakkai said to his students on his deathbed, "May it be God's will that His fear is upon you as is the fear of flesh and blood. . . ." The students asked in surprise, "Only as great, not more?" He replied, "Would that it be as great, for you know that when a man contemplates doing a sin, he says, 'I hope nobody sees me' (meaning people, not God). If men were conscious of being under God's scrutiny, they would not quickly sin." Rabbi Judah the Prince said, "Reflect upon three things and you will not come within the power of sin: Know what is above you, a seeing eye, a hearing ear, and a book in which all your deeds are recorded."[26]

The same practical principle is at the heart of rabbinic beliefs regarding the omnipotence and omniscience of God. The first refers to the idea that God is all powerful, and the second, to the idea that He knows everything. All of this is designed to give people the sense of having a Divine King, to convey the feeling that the world is a world of order and purpose and that people cannot escape the consequences of their behavior.

Among the many names used by the Bible and rabbinic literature to refer to God are *Father, Judge,* and *King.* In one sense, these terms tell something about the social and political attitudes of the people who used them. That is, for such people a stable society would be patriarchal, it would be a monarchy, and it would be characterized by the strong rule of law. But the terms also reveal that a leader was seen as being both very strong and very compassionate at the same time. In fact, rabbinic ideas about God (which follow directly from the Bible) stress these two divine characteristics. On the one hand, the rabbis insisted that God rules the world, that He controls nature and history, and that He is a judge who holds people accountable for their acts. On the other hand (and with even greater emphasis), they spoke of God as one who loves, becomes involved with, forgives, and cares very much about humankind.

Names are very important. Even today, we use names, particularly nicknames, to tell how we feel about a person. In ancient times, names were even more important. Often a name is used in the Bible (and in other ancient literature) to convey the essence of a person. The Bible uses two major names for God: *Yahweh* (usually translated as "Lord") and *Elohim* (usually translated as "God"). The rabbis taught that the former name reflects the quality of mercy or love and the latter name stands for the quality of justice or law. They pointed out that in the creation story of chapter one of Genesis, only the name *Elohim* is used, while in chapter two both names are used in describing the creation. From this they concluded that while God may have intended to govern the world through strict justice, He soon realized that He would have to mix His justice with mercy and love.

It must be obvious by now that the rabbis did not attempt to develop anything like a systematic theology. They were not interested in philosophy as an abstract discipline. Rather they were trying to teach people how to live in a difficult world. It is therefore not surprising to discover that God emerges in rabbinic thought as one who is transcendent (far above humans and the world) as well as immanent (very active in the world). Or as one who is considered to be omniscient (all knowing) and yet grants people the freedom of will so they can choose how to live. Or as one who is considered to be committed to both justice and mercy at the same time. It was not consistency that the rabbis sought so much as functional principles that may be used as guides for daily living.

NOTES

1. *Zohar*, Leviticus 73.
2. Genesis *Rabbah* 9:7.
3. *Tan. Pekude.*
4. *Mishnah Avot* 3:19.
5. TB [Babylonian Talmud] *Berakhot* 33b.
6. TB *Sanhedrin* 38a.
7. Authorized Daily Prayer Book, p. 10.
8. Leviticus *Rabbah* 34.
9. TB *Sanhedrin* 91a–b.
10. Leviticus *Rabbah* 4:6.
11. TB *Berakhot* 58a.
12. *Mishnah Avot* 3:11.
13. *Mishnah Avot* 2:1.
14. TP [Palestinian Talmud] *Nedarim* 9:4; Genesis *Rabbah* 24.
15. *Mishnah Avot* 1:14.
16. TB *Berakhot* 58a.
17. TB *Pesahim* 28b.
18. TP *Terumah* 8:4.
19. *Midrash Hagadol* Genesis, ed. S. Schechter, p. 189.
20. Genesis *Rabbah* 38:13.
21. *Mishnah Avot* 4:3.
22. *Midrash* Psalms 34.
23. Alphabet of *Ben Sira.*
24. Ibid.
25. *Mekhilta, Bahodesh,* Jethro 4.
26. TB *Berakhot* 28b; *Mishnah Avot* 2:1.

Part III

The Life Cycle of the Jew

Judaism does not have any sacraments, but it does observe certain rituals, which are considered to be *Mitzvot,* or commandments. These rituals do not have any cosmic or magical quality. Thus, for example, much of what happens in connection with death and burial is a result of *Minhag* (custom) that has gained the force of *Halakhah* (law) due to time-honored usage. The same may be said about the puberty rites called *Bar* (and, more recently, *Bat*) *Mitzvah*. Even the wedding ceremony, which follows a rather carefully prescribed ritual, does so essentially because it involves a change in legal status. As a result, Judaism, after the destruction of the Temple, never developed a clergy that would be charged exclusively with the sacerdotal responsibility of conducting the rites and ceremonies of the tradition. A rabbi is (literally) a teacher, one whose authority rests essentially upon his tested knowledge of *Halakhah* and *Minhag*. He is charged with the observance of the same *Mitzvot* as any other Jew—no more and no less. In many synagogues, particularly the most traditional, he does not conduct the religious services; this is done by any male Jew and—on special occasions, if desired by the congregation—by the *Hazzan* (cantor), an expert in liturgical music.

Time, to the Jews, is holy. They sanctify it. The high points in life are set aside and emphasized to give them special meaning. Part of this meaning is personal; but there is also a public aspect to these events, for the community is important in Jewish life. Thus each life-cycle event is not only a personal experience but one shared by the entire community.

BIRTH

Judaism has no distinctive ritual associated with the very first few days of life. If the new-born baby is a girl, the father goes to the synagogue on a day when the Torah is read (Sabbath morning and afternoon, Monday and Thursday mornings), is called to the Torah, recites the traditional benedictions before and after the reading, and then officially announces the name of the new baby.

Some Jews observe the custom of having a party in honor of the new arrival on the first Friday evening after the birth. However, there are no ceremonies associated with this occasion; it merely affords friends and relatives an opportunity of congratulating the father and mother (if the latter is not still in the hospital).

If the new baby is a boy, the naming of the child is part of a major Jewish ceremony—the *Berit Milah,* or circumcision. Contrary to popular belief, circumcision did not originate with the Jewish people. Many peoples around the world circumcized their sons. However, the Jews were the only ones to make this ceremony the visible "sign of the covenant"—the covenant made between God and Abraham and renewed in each generation through this ceremony (Genesis 17:9–14).

Because the original command to Abraham to circumcize his son specified the eighth day after birth, the *Halakhah* requires all healthy male children to be circumcized on that day. This is true even if the eighth day should happen to occur on a Sabbath or on Yom Kippur. The father is obligated to see that the circumcision of his son is performed, and he recites the following blessing at the ceremony.

> Blessed are You, O Lord our God, King of the universe, Who has made us holy through Your commandments and has commanded us to cause our sons to enter into the covenant of Abraham our Father.

The circumcision may take place anytime from sunrise to sunset during the eighth day. A quorum of ten adult male Jews, known as a *Minyan,* is usually present. The one who performs the operation is called a *Mohel.* He must be skilled in the necessary surgical techniques and must also be familiar with all of the Jewish laws that govern the ritual. It is customary to honor members of the family with roles in the ceremony. One member may bring the baby to the room where the *Berit* is held. Another may hold the baby during the operation. It is traditional to set aside a chair for the prophet Elijah, who is believed to be present "in spirit" at every *Berit Milah.* Following the ceremony, there is a meal in celebration of the performance of the *Mitzvah,* or commandment. Special prayers for the health and happiness of the new-born infant are added to the grace that follows every meal.

PIDYON HABEN

The ceremony fulfilling the command to redeem the first-born male child is called *Pidyon Haben* (redemption of the first born). This ceremony, which is scrupulously observed by traditional Jews around the world today, is biblical in origin.

> And every first-born male among your children you shall redeem. (Exodus 13:13; see also Numbers 18:15–16)

The Bible offers no explanation for this command, and the origin of the *Mitzvah* is obscure. A reasonable hypothesis suggests that the first-born male in each family was dedicated to the service of God. This dedication of the first-born male was the practice before the election of the Levites and priests to this service (Exodus 28:1). In order to release the first-born son from this service, he had to be redeemed by the payment of five shekels to the *Kohen* (priest), his surrogate. First-born sons of priests or Levites and of daughters of priests or Levites are exempt from this ceremony.

Like the *Berit Milah, Pidyon Haben* is an obligation of the father. The ceremony takes place on the thirty-first day after birth. If the thirty-first day falls on a Sabbath or a major holiday, the ceremony is postponed until the next day. The father recites a blessing and hands the *Kohen* "five shekels." Actually, the practice is to use the currency of the land, so that in the United States, five dollars would be given to the *Kohen*. The *Kohen* accepts the redemption money and blesses the child. The money is usually given to charity. The ceremony concludes with a meal of celebration.

BAR MITZVAH

At age thirteen a Jewish boy is considered by the Jewish community to be an adult. This means, on the one hand, that he is expected to perform the *Mitzvot* assigned to an adult male and, on the other hand, that he is granted full rights of participation in all Jewish rites and ceremonies. This major change of status is celebrated in a ceremony popularly known by the name of the new status achieved by the young man—*Bar Mitzvah* (literally, "son of the commandment").

The practice of accepting thirteen-year-old boys into the adult community is much older than the ceremony commemorating this change of status. The former is mentioned in the *Mishnah* (a portion of the Talmud); the latter may date from the fourteenth century. This ceremony takes place in the synagogue in the presence of a *Minyan*, the quorum necessary for public worship. The *Bar Mitzvah* youth is, for the first time, called to read a portion of the Torah and to recite the blessings before and after the reading. This represents public recognition of his new status. He is now accepted as a regular member of the community and is eligible to be counted in the *Minyan*.

For a period of a few months preceding his *Bar Mitzvah* ceremony, the young man is occupied with mastering the skills he is expected to acquire as a member of the adult community. He learns how to put on the *Tefillin*, or phylacteries, which are boxes containing bits of parchment inscribed with passages from the Torah. These cases, which are strapped to the forehead and the left arm, are worn by males during the weekday morning worship. If the *Bar Mitzvah* service is to take place on a Sabbath or a festival, the boy will probably be asked to chant the *Haftarah*, or selection from the Books of the Prophets. Since the *Haftarah* is chanted in a special cantillation which is hundreds of years old, he must prepare himself very carefully for this task.

In the United States, the *Bar Mitzvah* ceremony has assumed an importance that exceeds its role in the past. Typically, relatives and friends will gather to participate in the occasion. The *Seudah Shel-Mitzvah*, or ceremonial meal following the service, is often very elaborate. It may fairly be said that the *Bar Mitzvah* is a major event in the life of a Jewish youth and his family.

BAT MITZVAH

Bat Mitzvah (literally, "daughter of the commandment") is the status of a young woman who reaches puberty. Although many Jewish congregations have recently developed ceremonies to celebrate this occasion, there is no uniformity in the practices presently associated with them. Some congregations invite the girl to participate in a manner that exactly parallels the *Bar Mitzvah* service; others have developed a distinctive ceremony for girls.

CONFIRMATION

In the nineteenth century, Reform Judaism, the most liberal branch of Judaism, developed a confirmation ceremony that is uniform for boys and girls aged fifteen or sixteen. This confirmation was intended as a replacement for the *Bar* and *Bat Mitzvah* services. The idea of deferring the ceremony to a more mature age was to increase its religious meaning.

The confirmation ceremony gradually became associated with the festival of Shavuot. This association was based on at least three considerations: (1) Shavuot more or less coincides with the close of the academic year; (2) the confirmation could share the beauty and pageantry of the holiday; (3) the confirmation could be associated with the revelation of the Law at Sinai and represent a confirmation of faith in Judaism at the anniversary of this central event in Jewish history (see the section on Shavuot, pp. 80–81). In addition, the story in the Book of Ruth, which is read on Shavuot, was seen as a model of how one accepts membership into the Jewish people and hence as particularly appropriate for a service of confirmation. Although confirmation began as an alternative to *Bar* and *Bat Mitzvah,* it has become an additional celebration both in Conservative as well as Reform congregations.

MARRIAGE

The Jewish marriage ceremony is rabbinic in origin. The Bible does not indicate its nature.

The wedding takes place under a *Huppah,* or canopy. This is thought to be representative of the tent to which the bride was led by her husband in biblical times (Genesis 24:67). Others say that the *Huppah* symbolizes the home to be established by the new couple. In talmudic times, the wedding consisted of two parts, one of which *(Nissu-in,* or marriage) took place a year after the other *(Erusin,* or betrothal). Today, both ceremonies take place at the same time under the *Huppah.*

The wedding begins with the recitation of two blessings of betrothal. A cup of wine is then shared by the bride and groom. The Talmud dictates that the groom must give some object of value to the bride in the presence of two witnesses. Since the seventh century, it has been the universal practice among Jews for this object to be a ring. In giving her the ring, he declares, "Behold you are betrothed to me with this ring, according to the law of Moses and of Israel." This is considered to be the essential part of the wedding.

Next, the *Ketubah,* or marriage contract, is read aloud. This document spells out the responsibilities of the bride and groom for each other. It is signed by two witnesses, thus making it a legal document.

Seven blessings are then chanted over a second cup of wine, after which it is drunk by both bride and groom. These blessings sum up the ceremony and touch on the aspirations of the Jewish people. There is mention of Judah and Jerusalem and the revival of the nationalistic hopes of the Jewish people. This motif is carried through at the end of the ceremony when the groom crushes a glass under his foot. The origin of this custom is not certain, but for the past two thousand years,

it has stood as a spiritual reminder of the destruction of the Temple and of Jerusalem. Thus the custom fulfills the words of the Psalmist:

> If I forget you O' Jerusalem let my right hand wither; let my tongue cleave to the roof of my mouth, if I do not remember you, if I do not set Jerusalem above my highest joy. (Psalm 137:5–6)

Following the ceremony, a wedding feast is typically celebrated by the new couple and their family and guests. Celebrating the start of a marriage is considered to be a great *Mitzvah*.

DIVORCE

The fact that marriage is a human institution introduces the possibility of error. This possibility was foreseen in the Bible, which provides for a divorce ending the contract of marriage (see Deuteronomy 24:1–5, Isaiah 50:1, and Jeremiah 3:8). The nature of the divorce procedure, as with marriage, is rabbinic. Although divorce is permitted in Judaism, it is not encouraged. In antiquity, there was a difference of opinion between the school (disciples) of Hillel and the school of Shammai. The conservative school of Shammai held that adultery was the only grounds for divorce, while the school of Hillel maintained that divorce could legitimately take place for any reason. This latter view has prevailed.

The divorce proceedings take place before a *Bet Din* (Jewish court of law) consisting of three men who are knowledgeable in the Jewish laws of divorce. Also present are two witnesses and a scribe who writes the bill of divorce by hand according to precise rules and regulations. The bill of divorce, called in rabbinic terminology a *Get*, is then given by the husband to his wife. A woman may not remarry for three months after receiving a *Get*. Thus there can be no question as to the paternity of a child, should she remarry and become pregnant. Once divorced, her first husband may not remarry her if, in the meantime, she has been married to another and that marriage has been terminated either through death or divorce.

Jews are by their own tradition obligated to observe the civil law. This obligation is stated in the Talmud: "The law of the state is the law." Therefore, a *Get* is not granted until a civil divorce has been

A wedding in Jerusalem.
Attendants are holding the *Huppah*
over the bride and groom.

obtained, and remarriage is not possible unless the divorced person has obtained a *Get* together with a civil divorce. Just as the marriage had to be sanctioned by rabbinic law, so too it can be terminated only by the same authority.

DEATH AND BURIAL

Life is sacred in Judaism, and therefore the taking of life (except in self-defense) is considered to be a grievous sin. This strict position also applies to suicide and even to situations in which certain behavior would hasten the death of a dying person. Today, with new definitions of death emerging, serious questions are arising as to what constitutes justifiable behavior in such situations. Halakhists (experts in Jewish law), together with rabbis, doctors, lawyers, and ethicists (people who study ethical problems), are becoming increasingly involved in the study of such problems.

When a Jew becomes seriously ill and fears that death may be near, he or she recites a prayer that contains two elements: a plea for help in recovering and a confession of sins and of a desire to make good for all past misdeeds (the key phrase is "may my death be an atonement for all sins which I have committed"). The formula also includes the major liturgical statement in all of Judaism, the Shema: "Hear, O Israel, the Lord is our God, the Lord is One."

Judaism views the body as the work of God, and as such, it is respected in death as well as in life. The fundamental commandments pertain to washing and cleaning the body, honoring the body (it is not left unattended from death to burial), and accompanying the body to the grave. These commandments are considered to be especially meritorious since they cannot be reciprocated by the one who benefits from them.

Burial takes place as soon as possible, usually the day of death or the next day. This serves two purposes. First, it emphasizes the respect paid to the body, since leaving the dead unburied is considered to be a mark of great humiliation. Second, it is most considerate of the feelings of the mourners, since, to the Jew, the most difficult period for the mourner is the period between death and burial.

Jews have always chosen interment over cremation. The biblical basis for this choice is found in Genesis 3:19: "For dust you are and to dust you shall return." The dead are buried in shrouds made of white linen. This custom was instituted at the end of the first century C.E. as a way of eliminating a display of wealth at funerals. Linen was chosen because, at that time, it was the one material equally available to rich and poor. Among traditional Jews, the coffins used are simple and made entirely of wood.

The body of the deceased is prepared by washing and cleaning. No cosmetics are used, and the body is not embalmed, a practice that is foreign to Jewish tradition and usage. Every ancient and medieval Jewish community had a *Hevrah Kadishah,* or holy society, whose function was to prepare the dead for burial. Today, many Jews engage a professional funeral director, who arranges for all of the procedures involved in the preparation of the body for burial.

The funeral service is simple. Generally Psalm 90 and a memorial prayer, *El Male Rahamim* (O God, full of mercy), are recited. A eulogy is customarily given in honor of the deceased. During the service, the close relatives of the deceased cut a piece of the garments they are wearing as a sign of mourning. As they do this, the mourners recite a blessing: "Blessed be the righteous judge."

At the cemetery, the service continues with the recitation of Psalm 91, said as the body is borne to the grave, and of *Tzidduk Hadin,* an affirmation of divine judgment, given at the grave. The service concludes with these words:

> The Lord has given and the Lord has taken away, blessed be the name of the Lord. (Job 1:21)

The mourners then recite the *Kaddish,* a doxology or praise of God. Upon leaving the grave, those attending form two lines, facing each other. The mourners pass between them and receive words of consolation:

> May God console you together with all of the mourners of Zion and Jerusalem.

Although it is fitting for one to observe a period of mourning for the dead, protracted mourning is discouraged. There is a definite rhythm to the mourning period designed to balance respect for the dead with the gradual return of the mourner to a normal life. During the period between death and burial, the mourner is free of all obligations. Since even the observance of religious obligations such as prayer and study is suspended, the mourner is free to devote attention exclusively to the experience of mourning.

Following the funeral, a prayer service takes place in the mourners' home, followed by the *Seudat Havra-ah,* the meal of consolation. For the next seven days, a period called *Shivah* (seven), the close members of the family remain at home, sitting on low benches or stools as a sign of mourning. This period may be shortened to three days if the family is poor. During the *Shivah,* the mourners abstain from conducting

business and restrict their reading to books that are relevant to the mourning experience. They leave their home only on the Sabbath to join the congregation for services. During the other days, religious services, led by one of the mourners, are conducted in the home.

While it is improper to offer consolation during the period between death and burial, it is a *Mitzvah* to do so during *Shivah*. Thus relatives and friends come to visit and to console the mourners during this period.

After the *Shivah,* the mourners enter the period of *Sheloshim* (thirty). During this period, the mourners, while returning to their usual business, will generally avoid active participation in outside affairs. Entertainment is avoided during the *Sheloshim* and throughout the rest of the year. During the eleven-month period that follows death, the mourners recite the *Kaddish.* This prayer, while recited as an act of respect to the dead, makes no mention of death. It is a praise of God and the dedication of oneself to the perfection of the world. Reciting the *Kaddish* is considered to be a public declaration of the mourners' intention to carry on the ideals of the lost one in service to the goals of Judaism.

Each year, the anniversary of the death, called *Yahrzeit* (Yiddish for "anniversary"), is commemorated. The practices for this occasion include the kindling of a *Yahrzeit* candle, which is burned in the home for twenty-four hours and which serves as a symbol of the soul of the departed: "The candle of God is the soul of man." The *Kaddish* is recited in the synagogue. Some Jews also fast on this day. Today, Jews place a stone or marker on the grave. This may be done between 30 and 365 days after the funeral.

Finally, on the three major festivals of Passover, Shavuot, and Sukkot, as well as on Yom Kippur, the dead are remembered collectively at the synagogue service through the recitation of prayers which begin with the word *Yizkor* (may he remember) and the chanting of *El Male Rahamim* (O God, full of mercy).

A historic Jewish cemetery
in Prague, Czechoslovakia.

Part IV

The Cycle of the Jewish Year

The Jewish calendar is a lunar calendar; that is, it is based on the revolution of the moon about the earth. Months of this calendar have either 29 or 30 days, and the total number of days each year is 354. It is necessary to adjust the lunar calendar to the solar calendar so that Jewish holidays can be celebrated in season as required by the Bible. For example, Passover must be celebrated in the spring. The process of adjustment is accomplished by observing a leap year seven times in a cycle of nineteen years. Unlike the solar leap year, in which a day is added, the lunar leap year, called *Shanah Me-uberet,* requires the addition of an entire month. Thus during a *Shanah Me-uberet,* there are thirteen months instead of twelve. The added month follows *Adar,* the last month in the liturgical year, and is known as *Adar Sheni* (second *Adar*).

Prior to the establishment of the Jewish calendar in the fourth century, it was the policy to proclaim publicly the start of each new month. This was done by the religious leaders of the Jewish people and then conveyed to Jews in far-off communities. Since it took a while for the news to reach distant communities, the practice developed in such communities of adding an extra day to holiday celebrations. Thus, for example, Passover is observed for seven days in Israel but for eight days by most Jews in the Diaspora. Reform Jews, the most liberal of all Jewish groups, do not observe the extra day of each holiday.

THE SABBATH

The most important of all Jewish holidays is the Sabbath (Hebrew: *Shabbat).* It is a day of rest and is considered a sign of the *Berit* (covenant) between God and Israel (Exodus 31:16–17). The Bible gives two reasons for the institution of *Shabbat*. One is based on the creation story and the other on the Exodus from Egypt.

> . . . for in six days the Lord made heaven and earth and sea and all that is in them and He rested on the seventh day; therefore the Lord blessed the Sabbath day and hallowed it. (Exodus 20:11)
>
> And remember that you were a servant in the land of Egypt and the Lord your God brought you out from there with a mighty hand and an outstretched arm; therefore the Lord your God commanded you to keep the Sabbath. (Deuteronomy 5:15)

The Sabbath begins shortly before sundown on Friday evening and concludes shortly after sunset on Saturday evening. In the Jewish home, all preparations for the celebration are completed before the Sabbath actually begins. Much of Friday is devoted to such preparations as cleaning, shopping, cooking and baking special foods, as well as other personal preparations that one might expect before a major celebration.

The Sabbath celebration begins shortly before sundown, when the mother lights the Sabbath candles and recites this benediction:

> Blessed are You, O Lord our God, King of the universe, Who has made us holy through Your commandments and has commanded us to light the Sabbath candle.

The father recites the *Kiddush* (blessing over the wine and the Sabbath), which officially begins the Sabbath in the home. Following the *Kiddush,* all drink wine. Then, after a ceremonial washing of the hands, the following blessing is recited and the *Hallah* (Sabbath bread) is eaten.

> Blessed are You, O Lord our God, King of the universe, Who brings forth bread from the earth.

The Sabbath meal, the most elaborate of the week, may last a long time. Some families sing traditional Sabbath songs; others confine themselves to conversation. The total effect is to bring the family closer together and to foster a sense of family unity. The last official part of the meal is the chanting of the grace *(Birkat Hamazon).*

The next morning the family attends the synagogue as a unit. The service, a more elaborate version of the daily prayer service, consists of the recitation of prayers and a reading from the Torah and another from the prophetic books of the Bible. Usually there is a sermon delivered by the rabbi or someone designated by him.

After the service, the family enjoys another elaborate meal and spends a quiet day. Later in the day there is a third and final meal. Just

as the *Kiddush* begins the Sabbath, a service called *Havdalah* (separa-
tion) concludes the day. This ceremony consists of the lighting of a
braided candle, the drinking of a cup of wine, and the smelling of
spices, with appropriate blessings recited over each.

The importance of the Sabbath in Jewish life was summed up by
Ahad Ha-am, a twentieth-century Jewish philosopher, who put it this
way: "More than the Jew observed and preserved the Sabbath, the Sabbath preserved the Jew."

PASSOVER

Passover (Hebrew: *Pesah*) is one of three pilgrimage festivals
named in the Bible (the other two are Shavuot and Sukkot; see Exodus
23:14–16). On each of these festivals, the Israelites of old were to present themselves at the Temple "before the Lord." Each of the festivals
is associated with an agricultural event as well as with a historical or
religious event.

Originally, Passover marked the early spring harvest, which coin-
cided with the first full moon of the spring. The Bible also connects it
with the Exodus from Egypt (ca. 1220 B.C.E.). This connection, which
has almost completely overshadowed the agricultural one, provides
the dominant meaning of the festival for most Jews today. Thus while
the festival is called "the Holiday of Spring," it is referred to in the
liturgy as "the Season of Our Redemption" and "the Feast of the
Matzot (unleavened bread)."

During the pre-Christian era, animal sacrifices represented the
major form of Jewish worship; and on Passover, Jews sacrificed and ate
the paschal lamb. This practice ceased shortly after 70 C.E., when the
Jerusalem Temple was destroyed by Rome.

Eating special foods is still an important aspect of the Passover celebration. The major dietary restriction involves complete avoidance of
bread or any product containing leaven. This restriction is based on the
biblical story of the Exodus.

> The Israelites journeyed from Raamses to Succot, about six
> hundred thousand men on foot, aside from children. Moreover, a
> mixed multitude went up with them, and very much livestock,
> both flocks and herds. And they baked unleavened cakes of the
> dough that they had taken out of Egypt, for it was not leavened,
> since they had been driven out of Egypt and could not delay; nor
> had they prepared any provisions for themselves. (Exodus
> 12:37–39)

This experience was to be relived through the avoidance of leavened bread and the eating of unleavened bread by the descendants of the escaping slaves.

> Remember this day, on which you went free from Egypt, the house of bondage, how the Lord freed you from it with a mighty hand: no leavened bread shall be eaten. . . . Seven days you shall eat unleavened bread and on the seventh day there shall be a festival of the Lord. Throughout the seven days unleavened bread shall be eaten; no leavened bread shall be found with you and no leaven shall be found in all your territory. And you shall explain to your son on that day, "It is because of what the Lord did for me when I went free from Egypt." (Exodus 13:3, 6–8)

The center of the celebration of Passover is in the home. Elaborate preparations often involve every member of the family. The house is carefully cleaned before the festival. Since, according to the *Halakhah,* no leavened product may remain in the house, many Jewish families give the house a thorough spring cleaning at this time. Dishes and other utensils used throughout the year are carefully stored away and are replaced with utensils used exclusively during Passover.

In a quaint custom designed to dramatize the effort to rid the house of leaven, the children carefully deposit crumbs of bread in various parts of the house on the evening before the festival. To their amusement, the father then searches for the bits of bread. Before and after the search, the father recites a blessing and voices his determination to rid the house of all food judged unfit for Passover. All the gathered leaven is burned the next morning and thus, both symbolically and in actuality, the home is free of leavened products.

On the first evening of Passover and, for traditional Jews, also on the second evening, a unique meal and religious service are conducted in the home. As on the Sabbath and other major festivals, the meal is preceded by a candlelighting ceremony and attendance at the synagogue for the evening service. On this evening, perhaps more than on any other, the focus of the celebration is the meal and the service that precedes and follows it—the *Seder.*

The word *Seder* means "order." Its use derives from the fact that the service is governed by a strict order, faithfully followed by Jews for two thousand years or more.

The table is set with a *Seder* plate in front of each participant. Among the special foods on each plate is a roasted bone, symbolizing the ancient paschal sacrifice, and a roasted egg, recalling the festival sacrifice offered in the ancient Temple. These will not be eaten, but function as reminders of the Jews' links with the past. The other foods on each plate are to be eaten as the service progresses. These include three *matzot* (unleavened bread); *maror*, or bitter herbs, recalling the bitterness of slavery; a green vegetable, symbolizing the spring season of growth and renewal; and *haroset*, a mixture of nuts, wine, and apples, eaten to temper the bitterness of the *maror*.

There is so much to do during the *Seder*—foods to be eaten, wine to be drunk, songs to be sung, and the story of the Exodus to be read from an ancient book called the *Haggadah* (story of Passover). One highlight of the *Seder* is the asking of the "four questions," usually done by the youngest boy or girl at the table.

> Why is this night different from all other nights? On all other nights, we eat bread or *matzah*. Why on this night only *matzah?* On all other nights we eat all kinds of herbs. Why on this night only bitter herbs?. . .

In the middle of the service, there is an elaborate meal consisting of traditional Passover dishes.

The last part of the *Seder* consists entirely of prayers and of songs designed to end the *Seder* on a happy note. The final prayer expresses the hope of every Jew to be able to participate in the rebuilding of Jerusalem—"Next year in Jerusalem." With this, the *Seder* ends.

The *Seder* is an educational tool that involves the entire family. It employs virtually all the senses and mixes fun with serious learning and a sense of family togetherness.

SEFIRAH

The seven-week period separating Passover from the next classical Jewish holiday of Shavuot (Pentecost) is known as Sefirat Haomer (the counting of the *Omer)* or, simply, Sefirah (counting). The practice of counting the days of this period stems from a biblical injunction found in Leviticus 23:15–16.

> And you shall count from the morrow after the day of rest, from the day that you brought the sheaf of the waving; seven weeks shall there be complete; even until the day after the seventh week shall you number fifty days and you shall present a new meal offering to the Lord.

In order to understand the reason for numbering the days between Passover and Shavuot, one must understand that traditionally the two festivals have been viewed as inextricably connected. In fact, the talmudic name for Shavuot is *Atzeret,* or "concluding festival," signifying the link between the two holidays. Thus in counting each day from Passover to Shavuot, the Israelites were reminded of this relationship.

The counting started on the second day of Passover, the day on which the cutting of the barley harvest commenced in ancient Israel. On that day, an *Omer,* or measure of barley, was offered by each Israelite as a gift to the Temple in Jerusalem—thus the name "counting of the *Omer."*

As the biblical period gave way to the rabbinic period, Sefirah took on an entirely new coloration and became a period of semimourning. Jews have experienced much persecution, and thus it is natural that there are fast days and mourning periods built into the Jewish calendar. The connection of Sefirah with mourning is interesting because it reveals something about the nature of Judaism and of its particular value system.

During the second century C.E., the Jews rebelled against the Romans over the issue of religious freedom. The emperor Hadrian, seeking to create a more homogeneous religious atmosphere in the empire, had banned the rituals of Judaism (circumcision, Sabbath, dietary laws), closed the Jewish schools, and forbade the study of the Torah and of Jewish tradition. The rebellion was hopeless from the beginning. Yet the rabbis and their students felt constrained to fight because they realized that without schools and study, Judaism was doomed to extinction. During the war, many of the leading rabbis and scholars of Israel were martyred. The "armies of Israel" (actually students with no military experience or skills) fought an uneven struggle under the leadership of a charismatic general named Bar Kokhba.

The slaughter of these student-soldiers was such that the entire period between Passover and Shavuot is dedicated to their memory. During this period, Jews refrain from holding family celebrations or weddings. The major exception to this practice is Lag Beomer, the thirty-third day of the *Omer,* a day on which a victory was won against the Romans. Weddings are permitted on this day, and thousands of Jewish weddings are celebrated each year. In Israel on Lag Beomer, many Jews visit the tomb of Rabbi Shimon Bar Yohai who is said to have died on that day. He is believed to have saved himself during the Hadrianic era by hiding in a cave for thirteen years. He is also revered

Young girls garlanded with flowers
in a Shavuot procession in Israel.

as the reputed author of Judaism's most famous mystical work, the *Zohar*. Traditional observances of Lag Beomer include the reenactment of mock battles by children using bows and arrows, a playful recollection of a period of terrible warfare some two thousand years ago.

The commemoration of the Sefirah period, reminiscent of a war fought over freedom of learning and religion, symbolizes the central role of study and of the Torah in Judaism and Jewish history.

SHAVUOT

As indicated in the preceding discussion, the next classical Jewish holiday—Shavuot (Pentecost)—comes at the end of the period of Sefirah and is the concluding holiday of the Passover season. Literally, the word *Shavuot* means "weeks" or "feast of weeks." Its significance has both agricultural and historical bases.

Coming at the end of the Sefirah, Shavuot offered an opportunity for the ancient Israelites to bring the best of the new fruits to the Temple and to offer thanksgiving to God for their harvest (see Exodus 23:16 and Numbers 28:26). Each person who came to Jerusalem was to make a generous offering, as revealed, for example, in Deuteronomy 16:9–11:

> You shall count seven weeks from the days when the sickle is first put to the standing grain. You shall then keep the feast of weeks in honor of the Lord your God and the measure of your free will offering shall be in proportion to the blessing that the Lord your God has bestowed on you. You shall rejoice before the Lord your God with your son and daughter, your male and female servants and the Levite of your community as well as the stranger and the fatherless and the widow among you. . . .

The ritual and social concern shown here survived the biblical period and continue as major elements in the Jewish religion.

Gradually, in the postbiblical period, the emphasis of Shavuot shifted from agriculture to history. It became known as *Zeman Matan Torah* (the time of the giving of the Torah). The rabbis taught that it was on Shavuot that the Torah was revealed at Mount Sinai. This roughly coincides with the biblical statement that the Sinai incident took place about fifty days after the Exodus.

The talmudic name for Shavuot—*Atzeret,* or "concluding festival"—suggests more than a calendrical relationship between Shavuot and Passover. It points to a conceptual relationship as well. Passover is the holiday of freedom; Shavuot, the holiday of Law, or Torah. Judaism stresses that one is radically incomplete without the other. As the rabbis saw it, the Israelites were exchanging the arbitrary and heartless laws of an earthly ruler for the liberating laws of a benevolent God. Escape from the bondage of Egypt was necessary but incomplete. Without the Law, the rabbis saw people as slaves to impulse and whim, at the mercy of their feelings and instincts. It is the Law and its study which, said the rabbis, make true freedom and self-control possible.

In the celebration of Shavuot both the agricultural and the historical dimensions are still evident. The Ten Commandments are read in the synagogue before a congregation that rises in reverence. This ceremonial recreation of the revelation at Sinai is the highlight of the Shavuot service. The synagogue and the home are decorated with plants and flowers. The Book of Ruth, a beautiful love story with a harvest background, is read in the synagogue. In modern Israel, in addition to these customs, there has been a serious attempt to revive the connection between Shavuot and *Bikkurim* (first ripe fruits). Almost every village conducts some type of ceremony and the largest cities hold elaborate ceremonies. With song and dance, farmers from the surrounding areas bring baskets of *Bikkurim* to a central area, expressing pride and joy in the fruitfulness of the land of the Bible.

Jews observe another custom, called *Tikkun Leil Shavuot* (night liturgy of Shavuot), by staying up all through the night of Shavuot reading from the Bible, the Talmud, and other classics of Jewish literature. This ceremonial review of Jewish texts is another example of how modern Jews try to relive the ancient experience of the revelation of the Torah. (Note that the word *Torah* [literally, "teaching" or "law"] has been given an expanded meaning. Originally applied to the Pentateuch, or first five books of the Bible, it has come to be applied to all of the texts of Judaism.)

SUKKOT

The third of the three classical festivals is Sukkot, which begins on the fifteenth day of the month of *Tishri* (September-October) and lasts for seven days. As is true of Passover and Shavuot, Sukkot is associated with both agriculture and history. First, it is the festival of ingathering (Exodus 23:16), and as such it represents the climax of the agricultural year. But its name also points to a nonagricultural meaning: "You shall dwell in *Sukkot* [booths] seven days . . . that your generations may know that I made the Israelites dwell in *Sukkot*" (Leviticus 23:42–43). The historical connection refers to the fact that during their forty years of wanderings from Egypt to the Promised Land, the Israelites had no permanent homes. During this precarious period, they felt themselves to be under the protection of God, a protection symbolized by the *Sukkot*. On a functional level, Israelite farmers built *Sukkot* in their fields at harvesttime, so that they could spend as much time as possible in the fields.

The *Sukkah* (singular of *Sukkot*) was seen by the rabbis as a symbol of the fragility and transience of life. *Halakhah* requires that one who sits in the *Sukkah* must be able to see the sky through its roof, thus increasing one's awareness of the transitory nature of life and of people's dependence upon God through nature.

In Israel, virtually every family constructs its own *Sukkah*. Outside of Israel, while it is not unusual for a family to build a *Sukkah,* many Jews visit the *Sukkah* built outside a local synagogue. Given the harvest connection, it is not surprising that the *Sukkah* is decorated with fruits, vegetables, and other produce. Jewish families traditionally eat in the *Sukkah* during the festival, and some even sleep there.

The synagogue service during each of the seven days of Sukkot is marked with considerable pageantry. Four species of plants are used in the service: the *lulav* (palm branch), the *hadas* (myrtle branch), the *aravah* (willow branch), and the *etrog* (citron, which looks like an overgrown lemon and is highly aromatic). These four plants are tied together and at various points in the service are waved and carried in procession around the synagogue. This ancient custom represents a direct link between the modern synagogue and the Temple in Jerusalem.

This procession, during which the words *Hosha-na* (meaning "save us") are chanted, concludes the service on each of the seven days of Sukkot. On the seventh day, called Hoshanna Rabba, the synagogue is circled not once, but seven times to the accompaniment of the *Hosha-na* prayers. Then, according to custom, each worshipper holds small willow sprigs and shakes them three times so that leaves fall off, symbolizing the casting off of sins.

The conclusion of Sukkot is followed immediately by another holiday, called Shemini Atzeret. As previously pointed out, *Atzeret* means "concluding festival," and Shemini Atzeret occurs on the eighth day after the beginning of Sukkot. The synagogue service is marked by three special events. First, memorial prayers are recited as reminders

A Jewish family celebrating Sukkot dines in a decorated *Sukkah.*

of relatives, friends, and others who are no longer alive. Second, prayers for rain are recited. Despite the fact that most Jews lived outside of Israel after 70 C.E., the link with the land was preserved through the liturgy and celebration. Thus it is considered natural to offer prayers for adequate rain when such rain would be of greatest benefit to the land of Israel. Finally, the Book of Ecclesiastes is read. The somber message of this book provides an element of sharp contrast within the festival period, whose major theme is one of joy, thanksgiving, and optimism.

The second day of Shemini Atzeret (you will recall that an extra day was added to holidays outside of Israel) has a special name—Simhat Torah (the rejoicing of Torah). Over the course of one year, the entire Torah, or Pentateuch, is read in the synagogue. This cycle is completed and immediately started anew on Simhat Torah. Since the sixteenth century, the final reading has been preceded by processions in which the Torah is carried around the synagogue to the accompaniment of song, dance, and prayer. The atmosphere is extremely joyous. Following the last of the processions, the concluding section of the Torah, Deuteronomy 34, is read. The second reading begins the new cycle with Genesis 1.

ROSH HASHANAH

Rosh Hashanah (literally, "head of the year") takes place during the first two days of the month of *Tishri* (September-October). *Tishri,* which has more holidays than any other of the twelve months in the Jewish calendar, is the first month as years are calculated but the seventh month in the liturgical year, which begins in *Nisan* (March-April).

Preparation for Rosh Hashanah begins very early. In fact, the entire month of *Elul,* which precedes *Tishri,* is seen as a period of contemplation and self-evaluation. To contribute to this mood, two important additions are made to the liturgy. First, Psalm 27 is recited at the close of every service throughout the month of *Elul.* Second, the shofar, or ram's horn, is blown at the end of each morning service, a practice that is more universally observed during the week immediately preceding Rosh Hashanah.

As is true of all Jewish holidays, Rosh Hashanah begins at sundown. The celebration of Rosh Hashanah finds it greatest expression in the synagogue. Visually, the synagogue reflects the holiday. All vestments and ritual objects are white. The liturgy is lengthy and elaborate, touching on several themes. Some prayers stress the concept of history, since Rosh Hashanah is a time for reflecting on the events of the past year and of history; others deal with human deeds, for Rosh Hashanah is also a day of judgment. In one prayer, God is described as sitting on a throne examining the deeds of man, of nations, of all his creations. As the divine judge, God then decrees who shall live and who shall die. Judaism places a great emphasis on the idea that humans are creatures of free moral choice and can therefore be held accountable for their deeds. Thus the prayer ends, "But repentance, prayers, and deeds of justice can avert the evil degree."

The oldest ritual connected with Rosh Hashanah is the sounding of the shofar, as prescribed in the Torah.

> And in the seventh month, on the first day of the month, you shall have a holy convocation: You shall do no manner of work. You shall observe it as a day when the horn is sounded. (Numbers 29:1)

Three types of notes are sounded—some long, some broken, some staccato. The sounding of the shofar contributes to the majesty of the day and serves to stimulate a process of self-reflection. In addition, it evokes the traumatic story of the patriarch Abraham, whose willingness to sacrifice his son Isaac (Genesis 22) is an awesome example of faith and commitment.

YOM KIPPUR

Rosh Hashanah inaugurates a period of intense reflection and soul-searching known as the ten days of repentance. During this period, Jews make an effort to examine personal behavior and to take stock of their lives. The climax of the ten days of repentance is Yom Kippur, the Day of Atonement. The entire day is given to fasting, prayer, and contemplation. As with Rosh Hashanah, the celebration of this day is centered in the synagogue.

The theme of Yom Kippur is honesty and sincerity. The liturgy promotes a sense of the inadequacy of all human beings. None is perfect, all having committed sin. Two types of sins are recalled: those against God and those against other human beings. Of course, the two types overlap, but they differ in one respect. The Jewish tradition teaches that the experience of Yom Kippur—marked by repentance, charity, prayer, and other religious acts—can atone for sins against God. But, when one has sinned against another human being, one can atone for that sin only by seeking to make amends and to seek forgiveness from that person.

The synagogue service combines elements of the weekday liturgy and poems written especially for Yom Kippur, many of which were inspired by important events in Jewish history. In reading and chanting these poems, Jews recall their history and gain a sense of linkage with the past.

Unlike any other day in the Jewish calendar, Yom Kippur is celebrated in five services: the evening service (the holiday begins before sundown of the previous day), the morning service, the additional service, the afternoon service, and the *Neilah* service, which takes place at sundown. A final blast on the shofar, following *Neilah,* brings Yom Kippur to an end.

HANUKKAH

The festival of Hanukkah is celebrated for eight days beginning with the twenty-fifth day of *Kislev* (November-December). It commemorates the victory of Judah Maccabee and his men over native and foreign (Greco-Syrian) armies in Judea during the second century B.C.E. Though not biblical in origin, Hanukkah is extremely popular.

The Maccabean revolt, which is described in the apocryphal book of Maccabees, was led by a rural priest named Mattathias and his five sons, the most active of whom was known as Judah the Maccabee. The latter proved to be such an outstanding general that he was able to liberate the Temple, which the Greco-Syrians had made into a pagan shrine, and to reinstate the worship of God there. The elaborate rededication ceremony that followed this liberation provided the holiday with its name—*Hanukkah,* meaning "rededication."

Jewish tradition preserves the legend that it was impossible to find any oil that was fit for religious use in the aftermath of the rededication. This oil was needed in order to rekindle the eternal light (a feature of the Temple). The story goes that one small cruse of oil was discovered, enough to last for one day. Miraculously, the oil burned for eight days, and the holiday known as Hanukkah has been celebrated for eight days ever since.

A shofar is blown during the services
on Rosh Hashanah and at the conclusion of Yom Kippur.

In Jewish homes today, a special candelabrum is lit each night during Hanukkah. It is traditional to begin with one candle on the first night and to add another each night until eight are kindled on the last night. The lighting is accompanied by the chanting of blessings and the singing of songs. A popular game played on Hanukkah involves the spinning of a dreidel, a four-sided top marked with four Hebrew letters. The dreidel has been used by Jews on Hannukah since the Middle Ages.

PURIM

The festival of Purim (lots) falls on the fourteenth day of *Adar* (usually March). It is a biblical festival based on the story in the Book of Esther. The story tells of the attempt of an anti-Semitic Persian official named Haman to commit an act of genocide against the Jewish people. His plot was foiled by the efforts of Mordecai, a pious Jew, and his ward Esther, who had become queen of Persia. The name *Purim*, or lots, is derived from the fact that Haman is said to have drawn lots to determine on which day the slaughter would occur.

The central celebration takes place in the synagogue. At the evening service (and again on the next day at the morning service), the Book of Esther is read from a scroll. Each time the name *Haman* is read, a tremendous burst of sound erupts. Noisemakers known as groggers are used, and the usually dignified synagogue takes on a carnival-like atmosphere.

In Israel, the Purim festival includes a major parade in each city. It is known as an *Adlo-yada,* which means "until he is totally confused," referring to a tradition that on Purim one may drink to the point that he can no longer distinguish between Mordecai the hero and Haman the villain. Other Purim traditions include exchanging gifts, hosting a party, and giving charity to the poor.

Interestingly, the day after Purim (the fifteenth of *Adar)* is celebrated as Shushan Purim, because the people of Shushan, the city in which the story of Esther took place, observed Purim on that day. The practical significance of this is that all cities that were walled in ancient times and survive to modern times are to observe Shushan Purim (since Shushan was a walled city). Jerusalem fits this category.

The day before Purim is called the Fast of Esther, because Esther fasted before going to plead with the king to save her people. If the thirteenth of *Adar* falls on a Sabbath, the fast is observed on the preceding Thursday. With the exception of Yom Kippur, all fast days that occur on the Sabbath are deferred.

MINOR HOLIDAYS

Tu Beshevat

The fifteenth day of *Shevat* (January-February) has for two thousand years been celebrated as the New Year of the Trees, or Arbor Day. This coincides with the beginning of spring in Israel. The major customs of the day are the eating of some fruit that grows in the Holy Land and the planting of trees. In the early part of the twentieth century, the Jewish people established the Jewish National Fund to purchase land, to reclaim swamp and desert, and to plant trees in all the land of Israel. Millions of trees have been planted with these funds raised by Jews, particularly young Jews, around the world.

Yom Ha-atzmaut

The newest holiday in the Jewish calendar is Yom Ha-atzmaut, or Israel Independence Day, the anniversary of the signing of Israel's Declaration of Independence on the fifth of *Iyar* of 1948 (May 15). This holiday is very popular among Jews, not only in Israel but all around the world. For religious Jews, it represents the climax of two thousand years of prayer, hope, suffering, and effort. For all Jews, it represents the establishment of a home for all oppressed Jews.

Israel Independence Day is celebrated today in Israel and in Jewish communities around the world. Parades and other social activities are held. In special services held in the synagogue, the group of festival Psalms known as the Hallel (Psalms 113-118) is recited, together with special prayers on behalf of Israel. In addition, memorial prayers are offered for those who perished in the Holocaust and in Israel's war of independence.

MINOR FASTS

The twenty-four-hour Fast of the Ninth of Av (July-August) commemorates the destruction of Solomon's Temple by the Babylonians in 586 B.C.E. This act climaxed the destruction of the first Jewish state (see II Kings 25:3-9 and Jeremiah 52:12-13). In addition, other major calamities have struck the Jewish people on or near the ninth of *Av*. These include (1) the destruction of the Second Temple by Rome in 70 C.E., (2) the fall of Betar, the last Jewish fortress in the Bar Kokhba War of 135 C.E., and (3) the expulsion of the Jews from Spain in 1492.

This midsummer fast day climaxes a three-week period of semi-mourning that begins with the seventeenth of *Tammuz* (June-July).

This three-week period roughly coincides with the period of the final siege of Jerusalem by the Babylonians leading to the destruction of the Temple and the loss of Jewish freedom. During these three weeks, traditional Jews refrain from all celebrations. Weddings are not performed; new clothing is not worn. Some Jews even refrain from eating meat or drinking wine, except on the Sabbath.

There are three other minor fast days associated with the destruction of the Temple. These fasts, unlike the Fast of the Ninth of Av or Yom Kippur, are sunrise-to-sunset fasts, not twenty-four-hour fasts.

The Fast of the Tenth of Tevet (December-January) commemorates the beginning of the siege of Jerusalem by King Nebuchadnezzar (see II Kings 25:1; Jeremiah 52:4).

The Fast of the Seventeenth of Tammuz (June-July) commemorates the breaches made in the wall of Jerusalem during the siege (see II Kings 25:3-4; Jeremiah 52:6-7). These breaches assured the downfall of the city and the end of the first Jewish commonwealth.

The Fast of Gedaliah falls on the third of *Tishri* (September-October), immediately after Rosh Hashanah. On this date Gedaliah, the prince whom Nebuchadnezzar had appointed as governor of Judah, was killed (see II Kings 25:25; Jeremiah 41:1-2). This was the final blow to Jewish independence. The Fast of Gedaliah is the only Jewish fast day that is based on an event involving an individual, and there are no festivals in Judaism that are so tied to an individual.

There is reason to believe that the four fasts that stem from the fall of Jerusalem and the destruction of the Temple are very old. The Bible speaks of them in Zechariah 8:19:

> Thus says the Lord of Hosts: The fast of the fourth month [seventeenth of *Tammuz*] and the fast of the fifth [ninth of *Av*] and the fast of the seventh [the Fast of Gedaliah] and the fast of the tenth [tenth of *Tevet*] shall be to the house of Judah, seasons of joy and gladness and cheerful feasts; therefore love truth and peace.

Of the four fasts, it is the Fast of the Ninth of Av that retains the greatest hold on Jewish observance, perhaps because it has come to symbolize all of the national tragedies that have befallen the Jewish people throughout the ages.

An Israel Independence Day parade
in Jerusalem passing the old city wall
at the Damascus Gate.

Glossary

Aggadah (also spelled *Haggadah;* lit. "narration"). The nonlegal material in rabbinic literature, characterized by stories, legends, and proverbs, many of which emphasize morality and ethical behavior. Much of Jewish theology is found in the *Aggadah.*

Ashkenazi (pl. *Ashkenazim;* lit. "German"). A Jew of central or eastern European origin. In the Middle Ages, the Jews of Germany and France developed their own religious customs, rites, and culture. The center of *Ashkenazim* moved from western Europe to eastern Europe in the mid-sixteenth century. The *Ashkenazim* are generally compared and contrasted with the *Sefardim,* i.e., Spanish-Portuguese Jews.

Bar Mitzvah (lit. "son of the commandment"). A term for an adult male Jew. Upon reaching the age of thirteen years and one day, a Jewish boy has the responsibility to perform his Jewish duties according to the Law. Public recognition of his attaining this age is made by calling him to the Torah and by counting him in the *Minyan,* the quorum necessary for congregational worship.

Bat Mitzvah (lit. "daughter of the commandment"). A relatively new observance among non-Orthodox Jews, this ceremony is performed in recognition of a young girl reaching her age of religious responsibility on her twelfth birthday. Public recognition of her new status is made by calling her to participate in the congregational service.

Berit Milah. The covenant of circumcision whereby a male child enters into the covenant of Abraham (see Genesis 17:9–12). The rite of *Berit Milah* is performed on the eighth day after birth, even if that day is the Sabbath or Yom Kippur. During times of religious persecution when circumcision was forbidden, Jews chose martyrdom rather than leaving their sons uncircumcised. *Berit Milah* is to be postponed only on the advice of a physician. Once postponed, however, the circumcision may not be performed on the Sabbath or a festival.

Conservative Judaism. A religious movement of American origin which seeks to conserve Jewish tradition while adapting Jewish law to modern life. An outgrowth of Zacharias Frankel's Positive Historical Judaism, it is committed to the concepts of the people, the Law, and the land of Israel.

Diaspora (Hebrew: *galut;* lit. "exile"). The dispersion of the Jewish people after the destruction of the Second Temple in 70 C.E.

Essene. A member of an ascetic sect of the Second Temple period. Most Essenes lived in the Judean desert, forming religious settlements on the basis of joint ownership. The Essenes scrupulously observed the laws of ritual purity, especially ritual bathing. They not only withdrew from the rest of the Jewish people but shunned the Temple and its sacrificial system. Today many scholars identify the Essenes with the Qumran Sectarians, who inhabited the area where the Dead Sea Scrolls were discovered.

exilarch (Aramaic title: *Resh Galuta;* lit. "head of the exile"). The head of the Jewish community in Babylon, thought to be a descendant of the House of David. The office of the exilarch, dating from as early as the second century, lasted for about a millennium.

First Temple. The Temple built by King Solomon in Jerusalem. "First Temple period" is used to designate the era from the time of the Temple's construction to its destruction by the Babylonians in 586 B.C.E.

Gemara. From the Aramaic word meaning "to learn," it is the second part of the Talmud—the comments, explanations, and explications of the *Mishnah,* which is the first part of the Talmud. There is a Babylonian *Gemara* and a Palestinian *Gemara,* both based on the *Mishnah.* The teachers of the *Gemara* are called *Amoraim,* the interpretors of the *Mishnah.*

Haggadah (lit. "narration"). The liturgy of the night of the Passover; a book containing the story of the Exodus from Egypt together with an explanation of the symbols and rituals connected with the Seder service.

Halakhah. Discussion of the sages on matters of law and rules of conduct. *Halakhah* designates the legal material in rabbinic literature in distinction to *Aggadah,* which contains the ethical, story, legend, and moral aphorisms.

Hanukkah (lit. "rededication"). Eight-day holiday beginning on the 25th of *Kislev* (November-December). It commemorates the victory of the Jews over the Greco-Syrians which culminated in the rededication of the Temple in 165 B.C.E. The ritual consists of kindling candles for eight days.

Israel. The name by which the patriarch Jacob was known after his encounter with the angel (see Genesis 32:25–29). Also a name given to the northern kingdom after the split of the kingdom following King Solomon's death. Today the modern State of Israel.

Judah. Son of the patriarch Jacob; subsequently the name of the most important southern tribe from which the southern kingdom took its name after the split of the kingdom following the death of Solomon. Also known as Judea or Judaea.

Kabbalah (lit. "reception" [of Oral Tradition]). The mystical doctrines in Judaism.

Kaddish. A prayer; a praise of God recited at various parts of the synagogue service. In one form, it is recited by mourners during the year following the death of a relative and on the anniversary of the death.

Ketubah. The marriage contract, containing the mutual obligations of both husband and wife. The document is given by the groom to his bride. Originally it was a promissory note assuring the wife that in the event of the death of her husband or a divorce, a certain sum of money was to be given to her. Today it is mainly symbolic.

Kiddush (lit. "sanctification"). A ceremony introducing the Sabbath or a festival. It consists of two or more blessings over a cup of wine at the evening meal. It is likewise recited in the synagogue at the evening service.

Kohen (pl. *Kohanim*). A descendant of Aaron, brother of Moses, of the tribe of Levi. The *Kohanim* were the chief officiants in the Temple, offering the sacrifice and teaching the people the laws of the Torah.

Levite (Hebrew: *Levi;* pl. *Levi-im*). A member of the tribe of Levi. Levites were singled out to serve in the sanctuary as assistants to the priesthood in the capacity of musicians, singers, scribes, and teachers.

Maccabean revolt. See *Hanukkah*.

Messiah (lit. "one anointed with holy oil"). The redeemer who will come from the House of David and usher in an era of universal peace and prosperity in which Israel will be restored to its ancient land and way of life.

Midrash. The interpretation of the biblical text either to derive a moral or an ethical principle or to teach a law or legal principle from the biblical verse.

Minhag. The custom or usage which, although not derived from a legal enactment, enjoyed the same status as a law. It is said that "custom *(Minhag)* even takes precedence over law."

Minyan. A prescribed number; a quorum. The minimum number of ten adults required for communal service. A *Minyan* is required for the public reading of the Torah and the recitation of some specific prayers. Today many non-Orthodox synagogues count women in the *Minyan.*

Mishnah. Code of Jewish law compiled by Judah Hanasi, or Judah the Prince, about 200 C.E. It is the first part of the Talmud and consists of six orders, subdivided into tractates and chapters, each dealing with a specific aspect of life.

Orthodoxy. A modern designation for strict traditional Judaism which emphasizes divine origin of the Law and which demands adherence to the traditional law. Orthodoxy discourages any changes in the traditional law and prohibits any abrogation of it.

Passover (Hebrew: *Pesah*). Festival of Seven Days, beginning on the 15th of *Nisan* (March-April) and commemorating the Exodus from Egypt.

Pentateuch. Torah; the Five Books of Moses: Genesis, Exodus, Leviticus, Numbers, Deuteronomy.

Pharisee. A member of a religious-political group of the Second Temple period. The Pharisees considered both the Written Law of the Bible and the Oral Tradition to be authoritative in Jewish life. They were the precursors of rabbinic Judaism.

Pidyon Haben (lit. "redemption of the first born"). A religious ceremony conducted on the thirty-first day after the birth of a family's first-born male child, fulfilling the biblical law of Exodus 13:1–16. Both a Kohen and a Levite are exempt from this obligation.

priest. See *Kohen.*

prophet (Hebrew: *Navi;* pl. *Nevi-im*). An inspired person who spoke to the people in God's name as His messenger. "Prophets" likewise designates those books of prophecy which constitute the second section of the Hebrew Bible (Torah constitutes the first section and Ketuvim, or Holy Writings, the third).

Purim. A minor holiday; a joyous festival on the 14th of *Adar* (February-March), commemorating the deliverance of the Jews from extinction as described in the Book of Esther, which is recited on this holiday. Purim is marked by a carnival spirit involving parades, costumes, and revelry.

rabbi (lit. "my master"). A title of a sage or scholar; a term of honor. Today a title of one who is ordained by a rabbinical seminary or authority.

Reconstructionism. A movement, founded by Mordecai M. Kaplan, which defines Judaism as a civilization, stressing the peoplehood and its culture. Reconstructionism denies a belief in a personal, supernatural God.

Reform Judaism. A movement motivated by a desire to make Judaism conform to the needs of modern life. It emphasizes the nonlegal aspects of Jewish tradition and does not consider the traditional law to be binding.

Rosh Hashanah. Jewish New Year, celebrated on the 1st of *Tishri* (September-October); begins the ten days of repentance. Also called the Day of Judgment and the Day of the Blowing of the Ram's Horn.

Sadducee. A member of a conservative religious group made up of the wealthy and priestly classes of the Second Temple period. The Sadducees accepted the Written Law of the Bible as authoritative and rejected the authority of the Oral Tradition.

Sanhedrin. Greek name for a court of law during the Second Temple period. (1) The Sanhedrin Gedolah, which consisted of 71 members, met in Jerusalem and had jurisdiction over all religious matters. (2) The Sanhedrin

Ketannah (lesser court), which consisted of 23 members, met in the major cities in the land and had jurisdiction over civil and criminal cases.

Second Temple. Built in 516 B.C.E. on the site of the First Temple. "Second Temple period" designates the era from 516 B.C.E. to the destruction of the Second Temple by the Romans in 70 C.E.

Seder (pl. *Sedarim*). Festive, ritual meal eaten on the first night of Passover; observed also on the second night by Orthodox and Conservative Jews. The ritual consists of the recitation of the *Haggadah,* the narration of the deliverance from Egypt. The *Seder* table is set with special foods that convey symbolic meaning.

Sefardi (pl. *Sefardim;* lit. "Spanish"). A Jew of Spanish-Portuguese or Middle Eastern origin. The customs and rituals of the *Sefardim* differ from those of the *Ashkenazim.*

Sefirah. Sefirat Haomer, or counting of the *Omer;* the counting of seven weeks from the 16th of *Nisan* (March-April) until Shavuot, when the *Omer* offering of new barley was brought to the Temple. Shavuot falls on the fifteenth day of the counting and hence is called Festival of Weeks and, by Christians, Pentecost. In the rabbinic period, in the last days of the Second Temple, Shavuot celebrated the giving of the Torah on Mount Sinai, which, according to Exodus, took place three months after the departure from Egypt (see Exodus 19:1).

Shavuot. See *Sefirah.*

Sheloshim (lit. "thirty"). A period of thirty days of mourning observed by a relative upon the death of a family member. It is calculated from the time of burial. During this period all forms of entertainment are to be avoided. If a holiday intervenes during *Sheloshim,* the mourning is not continued, but ceases with the advent of the festival.

Shema (lit. "hear"). The first word of Deuteronomy 6:4: "Hear, O Israel, the Lord is our God, the Lord is One." The Shema is recited in the morning and evening prayer service. It contains three passages: Deuteronomy 6:4-9; Deuteronomy 11:13-21; Numbers 15:37-41.

Shivah (lit. "seven"). The seven days of mourning following burial. During the *Shivah* the mourner sits on a low stool and receives consolation from family and friends. *Shivah* is not observed, however, on the Sabbath or a festival. The mourner does not conduct business affairs during *Shivah* unless he or she would suffer severe financial hardship, in which case business may be conducted after the third day.

shofar. A ram's horn, sounded on Rosh Hashanah and Yom Kippur. On Rosh Hashanah three combinations of blasts are sounded: *tekiah,* a blast ending abruptly; *shevarim,* three short blasts; and *teruah,* nine staccato notes. The purpose of the shofar is to call the Jews to an awareness of the day, more specifically to the matter at hand—repentance.

Sukkot. A pilgrimage festival beginning on the 15th of *Tishri* (September-October); also called the Feast of Tabernacles or the Festival of the Ingathering of Crops. The festival lasts for seven days and is characterized by the *Sukkah,* or booth, a temporary shelter in which traditional Jews take their meals during the holiday. Four species of plants are used as symbols of the harvest: *lulav* (palm branch), *etrog* (citron), *hadas* (myrtle), and *aravah* (willow). In connection with the holiday, the eighth day, called Shemini Atzeret, is actually a separate holiday on which a special prayer for rain, called *Geshem,* is recited.

Tosafists. Talmudic scholars who wrote comments to the text of the Talmud and criticism of the commentary of Rashi on the Talmud.

Yahrzeit. The anniversary of the day of death. The custom of observing the *Yahrzeit* originated in the fifteenth century in Germany, from where it spread among Jews throughout the world. It is customary to light a *Yahrzeit* candle on the night before the anniversary date and to burn it until sunset of the following day. The custom is based on Proverbs 20:27, in which the soul is called "the lamp of the Lord."

Yom Kippur. The Day of Atonement, the 10th of *Tishri* (September-October); the climax of the ten days of repentance which begin with Rosh Hashanah. Yom Kippur is characterized by a twenty-four-hour fast, concentration in prayer, resolve to self-improvement, and petition for forgiveness of sin.

Zealot. A member of a Jewish sect that opposed Roman rule in the first century C.E.

Bibliography

History and Sociology

Abrahams, Israel. *Jewish Life in the Middle Ages.* Philadelphia: Jewish Publication Society of America, 1958. Also New York: Atheneum Publishers, 1969. An important study of the medieval Jewish community in Christian Europe, its institutions and life-style.

Eban, Abba S. *My People: The Story of the Jews.* New York: Behrman House, 1968. This survey of Jewish history by a distinguished diplomat and writer places special stress on the movements, both Jewish and non-Jewish, that affected the course of Jewish history.

Flannery, Edward H. *The Anguish of the Jews: Twenty-Three Centuries of Anti-Semitism.* New York: Macmillan, 1965. A readable account of the roots of anti-Semitism written by a distinguished priest of the Roman Catholic church.

Gilbert, Martin. *Jewish History Atlas.* Rev. ed. New York: Macmillan, 1976. A unique collection of maps dealing with every aspect of Jewish history.

Howe, Irving. *World of Our Fathers.* New York: Harcourt Brace Jovanovich, 1976. An interesting and comprehensive view of the Jewish immigrant experience in America.

Kaufmann, Yehezkel. *The Religion of Israel.* Translated by Moshe Greenberg. Chicago: University of Chicago Press, 1960. An important analysis of the relationship between biblical religion and the spiritual world of the ancient Middle East. It is particularly important for its discussion of the critical differences between monotheism and polytheism.

Klausner, Joseph. *From Jesus to Paul.* London: George Allen & Unwin, 1944. Also New York: Humanities Press, 1956. This volume on the development of Christianity as seen by a Jewish scholar discusses the ways in which what had begun as a movement within Judaism became a new religion.

————. *Jesus of Nazareth.* New York: Macmillan, 1957 (reprint of 1925 edition). A Jewish view of the life of Jesus, by a distinguished scholar of religion.

Levin, Nora. *The Holocaust: The Destruction of European Jewry.* New York: Schocken Books, 1973. A major study of the most tragic episode in Jewish history.

Roth, Cecil. *The Jews in the Renaissance.* Philadelphia: Jewish Publication Society of America, 1959. A bright chapter in Jewish history, illustrating the interaction of Jewish and Christian humanists and their mutual attraction to world culture.

Sachar, Howard Morley. *The Course of Modern Jewish History.* Rev. ed. New York: Dell Publishing Co., 1977. This book offers a highly detailed treatment of the events of the Holocaust and the birth of the State of Israel.

Shapira, Avraham, ed. *The Seventh Day.* New York: Charles Scribner's Sons, 1972. A moving account of the reactions of Israeli soldiers who participated in the Six Day War of 1967. It raises issues of the morality of war and explores issues of Israeli identity.

Sklare, Marshall, ed. *The Jew in American Society.* New York: Behrman House, 1974. This study by the leading sociologist of the American Jewish community discusses social characteristics of American Jews and their attitudes toward the family, Israel, and religion.

———. *The Jewish Community in America.* New York: Behrman House, 1974. This companion volume analyzes the Jewish community, its decision-making structure, religious movements, and relations with other groups in America.

Israel and Zionism

Elon, Z. Amos. *The Israelis.* New York: Holt, Rinehart and Winston, 1971. This book by an Israeli writer and thinker discusses the ideas, ideals, and problems of the generations involved in creating and maintaining a homeland for Jews in Palestine.

Herman, Simon. *Israelis and Jews.* New York: Random House, 1970. An important study of the ways in which Israelis approach issues of Jewish identity.

Hertzberg, Arthur, ed. *The Zionist Idea.* New York: Doubleday & Co., 1959. Also New York: Atheneum Publishers, 1969. A major source book on Zionism, with a superb introduction.

Holtz, Avraham, ed. *The Holy City.* New York: W. W. Norton, 1970. This book is useful in helping the non-Jew to understand what Jerusalem means to the Jew.

Philosophy and Religion

Agnon, S. Y. *Days of Awe.* New York: Schocken Books, 1965. Nobel Laureate, Agnon offers a charming collection of stories, customs, and commentaries on the High Holidays of Judaism.

Baeck, Leo. *The Pharisees and Other Essays.* New York: Schocken Books, 1966. A readable study of the Pharisees, their ideas and approaches to the interpretation of the Bible.

Bamberger, Bernard J. *The Search for Jewish Theology.* New ed. New York: Behrman House, 1978. An erudite but personal view of Jewish theology by a major leader in American Reform Judaism.

Belkin, Samuel. *Essays in Traditional Jewish Thought.* New York: Philosophical Library, 1957. A major Orthodox Jewish leader and scholar writes on problems facing America, commenting from a traditional Jewish viewpoint.

Blumenthal, David R. *Understanding Jewish Mysticism.* New York: Ktav Publishing House, 1978. A fascinating introduction to several streams within Jewish mysticism.

Bokser, Ben Zion. *Judaism: Profile of a Faith.* New York: Alfred A. Knopf, 1963. A leading Conservative Jewish rabbi and thinker discusses Jewish religion from both a historical and a personal viewpoint.

Donin, Hayim Halevy. *To Be a Jew.* New York: Basic Books, 1972. An Orthodox view of Jewish religion, dealing with observance of the laws and customs of Judaism and providing an Orthodox rationale for them.

Dresner, Samuel, and Siegel, Seymour. *The Jewish Dietary Laws.* New York: Burning Bush Press, 1959. A non-Orthodox approach to Jewish dietary laws and their meaning for modern Jews, including a guide to observance.

Millgram, Abraham Ezra. *Jewish Worship.* Philadelphia: Jewish Publication Society of America, 1971. A good introduction to the synagogue and the development of prayer within Judaism.

———, ed. *Great Jewish Ideas.* Washington, D.C.: B'nai B'rith, 1964. A summary of classical Jewish response to major religious questions. A special feature of the book is that the responses are written by representatives of every religious movement within Judaism. A discussion guide is available.

Moore, George Foote. *The Jews.* Cambridge, Mass.: Harvard University Press, 1927. A classical study of Judaism during the crucial period from 200 B.C.E. to 200 C.E., during which time the Pharisees and their successors, the rabbis, gave Judaism much of its lasting character. The author, a Christian scholar, taught religion at Harvard University for many years.

Schauss, Hayyim. *The Lifetime of a Jew.* Rev. ed. New York: Union of American Hebrew Congregations, 1976. A scholarly treatment of the life cycle in Judaism.

Steinberg, Milton. *Basic Judaism.* New York: Harcourt, Brace & World, 1947. A lucid and valuable discussion of Judaism and its most important beliefs and practices.

Reference

American Jewish Year Book. New York: American Jewish Committee.

Baron, Joseph L., ed. *A Treasury of Jewish Quotations.* Rev. ed. Cranbury, N.J.: A. S. Barnes, 1965.

Keikind, Miriam, ed. *Index of Jewish Periodicals.* Cleveland: College of Jewish Studies, 1963.

Patai, Raphael, ed. *Encyclopedia of Zionism and Israel.* 2 vols. New York: McGraw-Hill Book Co.

Roth, Cecil, and Wigoder, Geoffrey, eds. *Encyclopedia Judaica.* Jerusalem: Keter (distributed in the U.S. by Macmillan), 1972.